RAILWAY CENTRE YORK

A PICTORIAL AND HISTORIC SURVEY

Front Cover: With the magnificent York Minster forming the backdrop, a Gloucester Railway Carriage & Wagon Company Class 100 dmu passes an IC125 set arriving with a service from King's Cross on 12 April 1982.

RAILWAY CENTRE YORK

A PICTORIAL AND HISTORIC SURVEY

DAVID MATHER

PEN & SWORD
TRANSPORT

AN IMPRINT OF PEN & SWORD BOOKS LTD.
YORKSHIRE - PHILADELPHIA

First published in Great Britain in 2022 by
Pen and Sword Transport
An imprint of
Pen & Sword Books Ltd.
Yorkshire - Philadelphia

ISBN 978 1 39909 036 0

Typeset in 11/13 Palatino by SJmagic DESIGN SERVICES, India.

Printed and bound in India by Replika Press Pvt. Ltd.

Pen & Sword Books Ltd incorporates the imprints of Pen & Sword Books Archaeology, Atlas, Aviation,
Battleground, Discovery, Family History, History, Maritime, Military, Naval, Politics, Railways, Select, Transport,
True Crime, Fiction, Frontline Books, Leo Cooper, Praetorian Press, Seaforth Publishing, Wharncliffe and White
Owl.

For a complete list of Pen & Sword titles please contact

PEN & SWORD BOOKS LIMITED
47 Church Street, Barnsley, South Yorkshire, S70 2AS, England
E-mail: enquiries@pen-and-sword.co.uk
Website: www.pen-and-sword.co.uk

or

PEN AND SWORD BOOKS
1950 Lawrence Rd, Havertown, PA 19083, USA
E-mail: Uspen-and-sword@casematepublishers.com
Website: www.penandswordbooks.com

CONTENTS

ACKNOWLEDGEMENTS

With great thanks to my wife Mair for her continuing support and help with the manuscript and my good friend and railway enthusiast Rick Ward for allowing the use of his and his late friend Douglas Todd's photographs.

All photographs are copyright of the author unless credited otherwise.

CHAPTER ONE

THE STEAM ERA AND BEYOND

YORK STATION

'York . . . This is York' . . . the station announcer would proudly proclaim . . .
From the early days of the railways, York's history and development has been closely
linked with that of the personalities and companies responsible for the creation and
development of what was to become the national rail network. The construction of
the Stockton & Darlington Railway in 1825 led to a surge in interest in the economic
opportunities rail communication could bring and the prospects were not lost on the
citizens of York, one of whom was George Hudson. Hudson had been elected Lord
Mayor in 1837 and was not slow to use his money and influence in supporting the
building of York's first permanent station. Just inside the city walls, it opened on
4 January 1841 to be used only by the newly formed York & North Midland Railway
(Y&NMR) of which he was the Chairman. There had been a temporary station outside
the walls before this. A short time later the Great North of England (GNE) company
opened its line from Darlington to York, initially for goods traffic, but soon followed
by passenger services for which it negotiated the use of the station upon payment of
£5,000 towards its cost, together with further monies to be contributed for upkeep and
expansion.

As the railway system continued to expand, so did the fortunes of George Hudson as
he promoted and sponsored railway schemes throughout the country. In many people's
eyes he could do no wrong but by 1849 his methods were beginning to be questioned and
his reign as the 'Railway King' was soon to be over. His downfall was largely orchestrated
by his contemporary and successor as Lord Mayor of York George Leeman, who would
subsequently become Chairman of the powerful North Eastern Railway (NER), the
company which took over Hudson's original line, the York & North Midland, in the
amalgamation of 1854 along with the York, Newcastle and Berwick, the Leeds Northern
Railway and the Malton and Driffield Railway. Further additions to the NER empire
followed until the Hull and Barnsley Railway became the last to be incorporated in 1922,
the year before the NER itself would be subsumed into the London and North Eastern

Railway (LNER) as one of the so-called 'Big Four' created at the 'Grouping' of 1923, the others of course being the London, Midland and Scottish (LMS), the Great Western Railway (GWR) and the Southern Railway (SR).

The importance of securing a foothold in London was not lost on the ambitious promoters of early railways and several of the major players were competing for sites on which to build a territorial advantage. One such was the Great Northern Railway (GNR) whose Chief Mechanical Engineer Nigel Gresley would go on to achieve national fame in later years. Formed in 1846, its major objective was to build a line from London to York but doing everything possible to thwart this ambition was its great rival the Midland, whose creator George Hudson tried repeatedly to block the GNR's attempts to establish itself in the capital, forcing the latter to spend up to half a million pounds in Parliamentary and legal costs in its struggle to overcome the objections stimulated by Hudson. Once he had been defeated and disgraced as a result of his fraudulent activities, the GNR's goal could be achieved following approval by Parliament. By allying itself with the North Eastern Railway (NER) and the North British Railway (NBR), the Great Northern could now secure a main line north from London and beyond its previous extent of Doncaster, enabling seamless travel through York and as far as Scotland. The company began operating from London in 1850 after having hastily cobbled together a temporary terminus at Maiden Lane, spurred on by the urgent need to be operational in time for the following year's Great Exhibition in Hyde Park. The all too obvious inadequacy of this tiny station convinced the GNR of the need to expand into a bigger and better facility.

The location close to the Regent's Canal and to a junction of four major roads ensuring easy access was a major advantage. A statue of George IV erected soon after his death in 1830 and overlooking the position gave the area its name, King's Cross, which was adopted by the company. The new station was opened in October 1852 as the largest in Britain, even though its ten-acre site had only two platforms and no concourse but did have a fourteen track central section for parked carriages. Building costs were kept to a minimum due to the massive expenditure incurred in defeating Hudson but the design was undoubtedly influenced by that of the Crystal Palace, the centrepiece of the Great Exhibition. Nevertheless, the cost of the whole building was just £123,000, far less than for the earlier stations at Euston or Paddington and less than a third of what would later be spent creating a new station at York.

Hudson's station at York had one major disadvantage – it was a terminus accessed through an arch in the city walls. In the early days when traffic was light this could be managed easily by reversing trains or by locos running round their coaches before continuing their journey. However, as time passed and traffic increased, it became apparent that additional systems needed to be put into operation. These included the construction of 'ticket platforms' outside the station where tickets could be checked while the locomotive was being detached to run round its train, which would then be propelled into the station platform. Additional platforms were also constructed at Holgate Bridge in the 1860s for use at particularly busy times such as during York race meetings. These became known locally as the Racecourse Station and continued in operation until August 1939 under their correct title of Holgate Extension Platforms. The buildings survived until 1962, when they were eventually demolished.

It was in July 1866 that plans for a new 'through' station at York were sanctioned by Act of Parliament and the troublesome and potentially hazardous procedures of reversals and run-rounds would become a thing of the past. The 'new' station, as opened on 25 June 1877 with its imposing curved roof rising high above the through platforms, was described as 'the finest and largest structure of its kind in the world'.

York's first permanent station, inside the City Walls, opened on 4 January 1841 for the York & North Midland Railway. The 'New Station' would be opened some thirty-six years later with an impressive thirteen platforms. The pride of the North Eastern Railway, it was at the time the largest railway station in the world.

This came at a cost estimated at the time to be in the region of £400,000 (today equivalent to about £50m) and though it was wholly owned by the North Eastern Railway, some revenue was recouped by the rental fees paid by other companies for use of the facilities. These included the Midland, Great Northern, Lancashire & Yorkshire, Great Eastern, London & North Western and the Great Central railway companies, and with this rapidly expanding use came the need for increased servicing facilities which were provided in the form of large locomotive sheds at each end of the new station ('York North' and 'York South') and extensions to the locomotive repair shops of the former Y&NMR. That company had previously relied on a small shed which was demolished to make way for the new station, and five further sheds were built on land formed by the line into the old station and the North Junction – Holgate Bridge Junction curve. These, known as York South, consisted of three roundhouses and two straight sheds, the first opening in about 1850. The first two roundhouses had sixteen stalls served by a forty-two foot turntable while the larger third roundhouse added in 1864 had eighteen stalls and a forty-five foot turntable.

Standing outside York South shed c.1960 is Worsdell J72 0-6-0T number 68677, a product of Darlington Works from December 1900. She was transferred to York North shed when York South was to be closed only to be withdrawn in October 1961 and cut up at Darlington North Road Works shortly afterwards.

In 1878, a large shed to be known as York North, Clifton or Leeman Road was completed beside the line to the north of the station. This consisted of three roundhouses for sixty engines to which a fourth with a sixty-foot turntable was added in 1915, along with a new coaling stage. In spite of these enlarged facilities, York still had no turntable large enough for turning the largest locomotives which had begun to operate through the city since the early 1920s, these having to be turned using the Holgate Junction-North Junction-Clifton Junction triangle until in 1932 a seventy-foot electric turntable was completed in the shed yard. In anticipation of receiving allocations of 4-6-2 'Pacific' engines in the mid-1930s, Number Four shed was also upgraded by the installation of a seventy-foot turntable. These superior facilities being developed at York North shed promoted its further growth while the importance of its 'little sister' South shed diminished, resulting in closure in 1961 and it was finally demolished in 1963.

From 1954, Number One and Number Two roundhouses at York North were demolished and replaced by a straight shed, while Number Three and Number Four were rebuilt retaining their original turntables, only to be closed with the demise of steam in 1967. York's allocation of diesel locos was relocated to the straight shed while the surviving roundhouses were made available to house the new National Railway Museum, opened in 1975. The diesel depot closed in 1982 when that building too was taken over by the museum, resulting in the remaining locos being stabled in the sidings outside.

In spring, the ramparts opposite the station are covered with daffodils welcoming the traveller to this ancient city while below, through a nearby arch in the wall, evidence of the original station's platform can still be seen.

The most complete medieval city walls in England offer an opportunity to view the exterior of the station built in yellow Scarborough brick and with the former Royal Station Hotel, now the York Principal, on the right. The original Royal Station Hotel was adjacent to the original station within the city walls and is now used as offices. The large clock visible on the portico is very characteristic of the North Eastern Railway and matches the one within the station at the end of the footbridge.

Within the station can be found numerous reminders of the railway's past:

Next to the footbridge outside what was the station signal box can be seen the Coat of Arms of the North Eastern Railway along with the White Rose of Yorkshire and above them still in place are signal wire pulleys dating back to a time when semaphore signals controlled traffic through the station.

The 'new' station at York became the hub of the NER system and the company's headquarters was established nearby in the city. Its design recalls Brunel's station at Paddington, the ultimate cathedral of steam with its wrought iron arches, though York's supporting arcades are more substantial. The ornate ironwork throughout the station recalls its origins though the original roof was timber clad with slates and skylights.

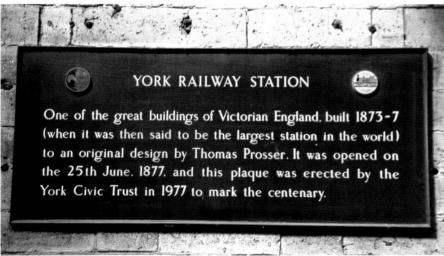

YORK RAILWAY STATION

One of the great buildings of Victorian England. built 1873-7 (when it was then said to be the largest station in the world) to an original design by Thomas Prosser. It was opened on the 25th June. 1877. and this plaque was erected by the York Civic Trust in 1977 to. mark the centenary.

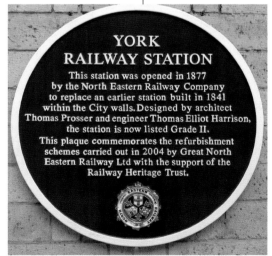

YORK RAILWAY STATION
This station was opened in 1877 by the North Eastern Railway Company to replace an earlier station built in 1841 within the City walls. Designed by architect Thomas Prosser and engineer Thomas Elliot Harrison, the station is now listed Grade II.
This plaque commemorates the refurbishment schemes carried out in 2004 by Great North Eastern Railway Ltd with the support of the Railway Heritage Trust.

Above left and above right: This plaque commemorating the station's centenary was later replaced by the circular one.

Left: The station facilities were greatly improved with the opening of the new Travel Centre in 1984.

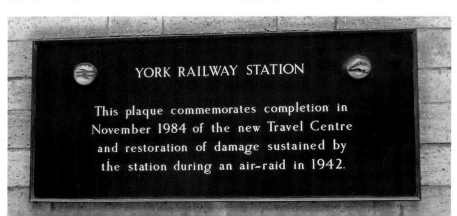

YORK RAILWAY STATION

This plaque commemorates completion in November 1984 of the new Travel Centre and restoration of damage sustained by the station during an air-raid in 1942.

An impressive tiled map of the North Eastern Railway adorns the inner wall of the station.

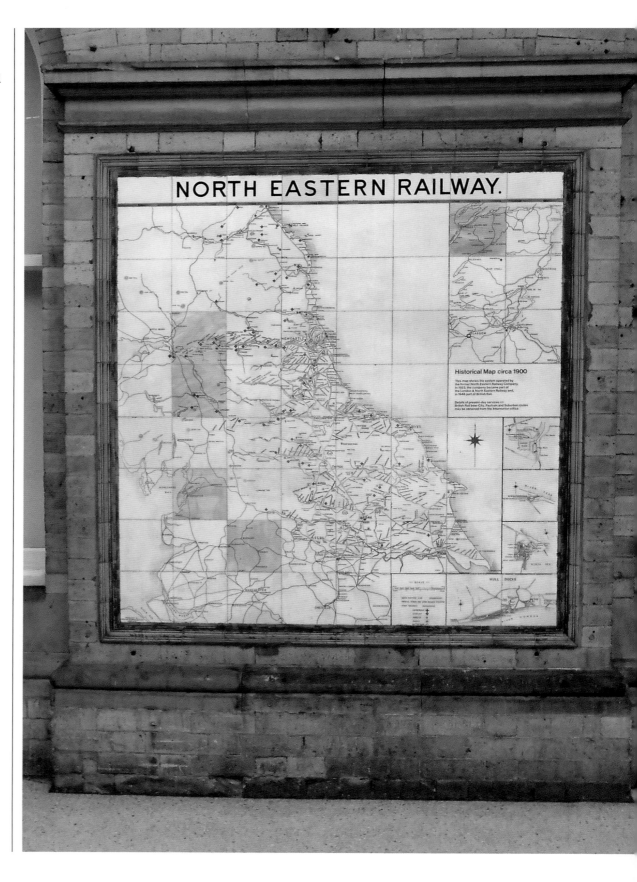

One of the few examples of an NER 'slotted' lower quadrant semaphore distant signal is preserved within the station concourse, this one rescued from the York to Scarborough line near Haxby in 1984. Unlike the yellow with black chevron generally adopted from the 1920s for distant signals, the NER opted for the red and white colour scheme shown.

In addition to the familiar mileposts positioned along the tracks, each station on the North Eastern Railway was marked by a Datum Post or Distance Post to show the point from which the distance along each route or branch was measured. This 'Zero Post' is a replica of the original which was lost from the station, possibly during clearing up after the Second World War bombing raid of April 1942. It carries ten tablets referring to the branches measured from here, namely Longlands Loop (Northallerton), Market Weighton and Beverley, Micklefield Branch (Church Fenton to Micklefield), Raskelf Curve, Sherburn Branch (Sherburn Junction to Gascoigne Wood Junction), York and Harrogate, York and Market Weighton, York and Newcastle, York and North Midland (York to Altofts Junction near Normanton) and York and Scarborough.

50A YORK NORTH DEPOT

Such was the importance of York North motive power depot, coded 50A in the BR steam era, that from the late 1940s it was home to over 200 steam locomotives, more than half of which were mixed traffic engines largely made up of LNER class B16 4-6-0s designed by Vincent Raven and introduced from 1920 as NER class S3, together with substantial numbers of Gresley V2 2-6-2s and a few Thompson B1 4-6-0s. A handful of express passenger locos from Peppercorn's A1 and A2 classes also graced the shed, but the remainder consisted of an assortment of 0-6-0 freight locos mainly representing classes J21, J71, J72 and J94. Also present were a small number of BR class 4 and 5s and ten WD 8Fs. By the mid-1960s, as the end of steam approached, the allocation had changed considerably. Gone were most of the 0-6-0 freight locos having been replaced by diesel shunters of classes 03, 04 and 08, though some former NER B16s still survived, as did an increased allocation of LNER A1, B1 and V2 engines, together with new additions from class K1 and BR class 9F 2-10-0s. The rest of the allocation of 166 locos comprised mainly the new generation of diesel locos of which the class 40s were the most numerous with thirty-three examples. Throughout the 1960s, York's steam locomotives could be seen simmering between duties outside the depot, working through the station or on very rare occasions might be spotted within North Shed itself.

A shed plate as carried on the smoke box door of one of York North's steam locomotives.

Around a turntable in York North shed in 1963 are Worsdell 5F class J27 0-6-0 number 65894 built at Darlington Works in 1923, a visitor from Darlington mpd (51A) BR 3MT 2-6-2T number 82029 built at Swindon Works in 1954, and Thompson B1 4-6-0 number 61288 built by the North British Locomotive Company, Glasgow in 1948. Number 65894 was withdrawn from service on 30 September 1967 but was saved into preservation by the North Eastern Locomotive Preservation Group and is currently based on the North Yorkshire Moors Railway, having been returned to service in May 2018 following a twelve-year overhaul. Number 82029 was withdrawn on 9 July 1967 and cut up at Bird's scrapyard, Risca, Newport, Monmouthshire in January 1968. Number 61288 was withdrawn on 6 January 1964 and cut up soon after at BR's Darlington North Road Works.

Within York North shed during 1965 are Ivatt 4F-A 2-6-0 number 43138, built at Doncaster Works during July 1951 and withdrawn from shed 52F North Blyth in April 1967 to be scrapped soon after by Arnott Young at Dinsdale. Next to her is Worsdell J27 0-6-0 number 65894, built at Darlington Works in September 1923 and withdrawn from shed 54A Sunderland South Dock during September 1967. She is now preserved and working on the North Yorkshire Moors Railway. Third from the left is Thompson B1 4-6-0 number 61021 *Reitbok*, built at Darlington Works in March 1947 and withdrawn from York North shed in June 1967 to be scrapped at Hughes Bolckon's Battleship Wharf yard, North Blyth in August the same year. Finally, around the turntable is Ivatt 4F-A 2-6-0 number 43071, another product of Darlington Works from August 1950 this time. Like her sister to the left, she too was withdrawn from shed 52F North Blyth during the spring of 1967 and sent to the same yard for scrapping later that year.

In York North shed during 1966 are two very different products of the North British Locomotive Company's Glasgow Works. Stanier LMS Jubilee 4-6-0 number 45562 *Alberta* stands alongside Peppercorn K1 2-6-0 number 62012. Built in 1934, the Jubilee was visiting from Leeds Holbeck shed, 20A, from where she was withdrawn on 4 November 1967 to be cut up at Cashmore's scrap-yard, Great Bridge, in May 1968 while the 1949 vintage K1, carrying a York North shed-plate, 50A, was withdrawn on 31 May 1967 and suffered a similar fate at Draper's Neptune Street Goods Yard, Hull in August 1967.

In the Repair Shops at York depot during April 1964 is Gresley V2 2-6-2 number 60941, built at Darlington Works in March 1942. A long-term resident of shed 50A York North, one wonders if her repairs were ever completed as she was withdrawn from service on 6 July 1964 to be cut up at Swindon Works.

The view of parked or withdrawn locomotives waiting in the sidings outside York North shed was often obscured by parked trucks. Here in the 1960s, a couple of Thompson B1s and a Raven Q6 0-8-0 await their fate.

Simmering between turns outside her home shed York North on 11 March 1962, is Thompson rebuild B16/3 of Raven B16/1 4-6-0 number 61467. Originally built at Darlington Works in 1924 with inside Stephenson gear, she was rebuilt in 1944 with three Walschaerts gears. She survived until 30 June 1964, when she was withdrawn and cut up at Draper's Neptune Street Goods Yard, Hull later that year.

Looking well in York North shed yard during 1962 is Gresley class A3 7P6F 4-6-2 number 60054 *Prince of Wales*. Built at Doncaster Works in 1924 as LNER class A1, later A10, she was rebuilt in July 1943 and was withdrawn from shed 34F Grantham on 28 June 1964 to be cut up later that year at A. King & Sons Ltd, Norwich.

At the buffers in her home shed yard, York North c. 1961, is Thompson A2/3 4-6-2 number 60515 *Sun Stream*. Built at Doncaster Works in 1946 as a development of Thompson's A2/2 but with double chimney, she worked until her withdrawal on 12 November 1962 when she was returned to Doncaster Works to be cut up in April 1963.

With York North shed's imposing coaling stage in the background, Worsdell class J27 0-6-0 number 65873 stands condemned in the yard on 16 February 1967. Built at Darlington Works in 1922, she worked out of Sunderland mpd, 52G, until being withdrawn on 31 October 1966 and later transferred to Draper's Neptune Street Goods Yard where she was cut up in May 1967.

Awaiting transfer to BR's Darlington North Road Works for disposal, Worsdell class J72 0-6-0T number 68752 stands in the yard at York c.1960. Built at Doncaster Works in 1925, she spent most of her life working in the Hull area from shed 53C Hull Springhead until being withdrawn on 29 February 1960 for scrapping.

Worsdell J72 0-6-0T number 69020 waits out of service at York North shed in 1959. Built in 1950 at Darlington Works, she worked out of shed 50B Hull Dairycoates until being transferred to 51A Darlington prior to withdrawal on 31 December 1963, following which she was cut up at T.J. Thompson & Sons scrap-yard, Stockton during January 1965. Alongside is sister loco number 69003, withdrawn at the same time.

The sidings are busy as Gresley A3 number 60090 *Grand Parade* approaches York North depot in 1960. Built at Doncaster Works in August 1928, she was badly damaged in an accident at Castlecary, North Lanarkshire in January 1937 and was taken back to Doncaster Works where she was rebuilt from spare parts. Her final shed was 65B St. Rollox from where she was withdrawn on 28 October 1963 to be sent to BR's Cowlairs Works for disposal, being cut up during January 1964.

Coming on shed at York North in the early 1960s is Stanier 8F 2-8-0 number 48427, built at Swindon Works in January 1944. Withdrawn in August 1965, she was scrapped the same year. In the background waits the next generation in the shape of English Electric Type 4 number D351 (later 40 151). One of 200 such diesels built between 1958 and 1962, she too would be withdrawn and scrapped some twenty years later.

Gresley V2 number 60831 stands amongst the redundant locos in York North yard, her home shed, in 1966. Built at Darlington Works in 1938, she was withdrawn from service on 6 December 1966 and scrapped at Draper's Neptune Street Goods Yard, Hull during February 1967.

Coming onto the shed at York North after bringing in her train on 7 August 1965 is BR Class 5 4-6-0 number 73137 of Patricroft shed, 10C. Built at Derby Works during 1956, she was withdrawn on 30 June 1967 to be scrapped at Cashmore's scrap-yard, Great Bridge during January 1968. She is seen passing a smartly turned out Stanier 8F 2-8-0 number 48622, a product of Ashford Works on the former Southern Railway where she was built in November 1943. She was withdrawn in November 1967 from shed 55B Stourton to be cut up the following year.

Leaving York station for North shed on 5 May 1964 is WD 'Austerity' 8F number 90480. Designed by Riddles for the Ministry of Supply and built at Vulcan Foundry during June 1944, she was withdrawn from shed 36A Doncaster on 31 July 1965, to be cut up at W. George & Son's Station Steel scrap-yard, Wath-on-Dearne during September 1965.

Passing the 'Racecourse Station' at Holgate, LNER B16/3 number 61476 approaches York in the 1950s. Built in March 1920 and rebuilt by Thompson in 1944, her final shed was 25D Mirfield from where she was withdrawn on 30 September 1963 to be cut up at Darlington North Road Works later that year.

Passing Holgate and approaching York station on 15 July 1965 is Hughes 2-6-0 'Crab' number 42938, a product of Crewe Works during 1932. She spent much of her working life operating out of shed 9B Stockport Edgeley but was transferred to 26A Newton Heath from where she was withdrawn on 25 September 1965 to be cut up at T.W. Ward's scrap-yard at Beighton, Sheffield during December the same year.

At the platform at York station on 2 April 1959 stands Gresley A2 number 60502 *Earl Marischal* with her unusual chimney smoke deflectors. Built at Doncaster Works in 1934 and rebuilt by Thompson in 1943, she was withdrawn from York North shed in July 1961 to be returned to Doncaster Works for disposal.

Gresley A3 4-6-2 number 60072 *Sunstar* passes through York station with a dynamometer car attached, c.1951. Built during September 1924 at North British Locomotive Works, Glasgow, her last shed was 52B Heaton from where she was withdrawn on 22 October 1962 and cut up at Doncaster Works during May 1963.

Racing along the ECML in early 1963 is Gresley A4 4-6-2 number 60025 *Falcon*. Built at Doncaster Works during 1937 she graced the tracks from King's Cross shed, 34A, but was withdrawn from service on 20 October 1963 to return to Doncaster Works for disposal, which took place during January 1964.

The end of the line. Peppercorn A1 4-6-2 number 60146 *Peregrine* stands at her home depot York North, 50A, awaiting disposal on 10 October 1965. Built at Darlington Works on 11 April 1949 she was withdrawn on 4 October 1965, less than a week before this photo was taken. Her final movement would be to T.W. Ward's scrapyard at Killamarsh, Derbyshire where she was cut up during November of the same year.

With the end of steam approaching, the era of the charter special was upon us. Here, Stanier Jubilee 4-6-0 number 45565 *Victoria* storms away from York with train 1X50, the Altrinchamian Railway Excursion Society 'Waverley Special' on 23 April 1966. This was the society's first rail-tour and ran from Manchester Exchange station via the West Coast Main Line to Carlisle then on to Edinburgh Waverley via the Waverley Route, with Peppercorn A2 number 60528 *Tudor Minstrel* in charge. The leg from Edinburgh Waverley to Berwick-upon-Tweed was headed by Gresley V2 number 60836 and from Berwick to York sister loco number 60824 was at the front. Finally it was the turn of the Jubilee, with 45565 taking the tour back from York to Manchester Exchange. She was built in 1934 by the North British Locomotive Company, Glasgow and worked for many years out of Leeds Holbeck shed, coded 20A, before being withdrawn on 6 January 1967 and sent for scrapping to Draper's Neptune Street Goods Yard, Hull, completed in June 1967.

By the end of 1965 steam was in rapid retreat in the north east of England, though a few loco sheds in this area did still hang on to a handful of survivors. York, Hull and Leeds Neville Hill were among those offering them a home while further north Tweedmouth, Blyth, Tyne Dock, Sunderland, West Hartlepool and Darlington depots continued to function. It was the closure of Darlington North Road Works, scheduled for April 1966, that signalled that the end of steam in the region was truly near, for with the demise of this repair facility any major parts failure would herald the withdrawal and scrapping of the loco concerned.

So it was that BR announced that the final scheduled steam-hauled express passenger train in the north east would run on New Year's Eve, 31 December 1965, between York and Newcastle. The loco involved was the last surviving Peppercorn A1 Pacific number 60145 *Saint Mungo*. Many enthusiasts turned out to witness the event and as no speed limit for steam traction was then in force the loco was given its head on the return journey and achieved 100mph (161km/h) before reaching York. Sadly though, in those days the preservation of steam locomotives was largely a dream and within six months *Saint Mungo* had been sent for scrap.

YORK'S WIDER RAILWAY HERITAGE

Of major importance when considering the railway heritage of York was the Carriage Works in Holgate. The North Eastern Railway (NER) had workshops in York from 1842 and a repair facility for wagons was added later in 1865. The Holgate Road site was opened in 1884 as a carriage building workshop for the NER and continued in this role in LNER and British Railways ownership, at that time employing around 5,000 people. In the 1980s, the works was extensively modernised, resulting in a series of labour-saving manufacturing methods being introduced and consequently reducing the workforce dramatically. In addition to carriage building, diesel and electric multiple units (dmus and emus) for home and abroad were manufactured here, including the Class 150 dmu, 'Networkers' for Network SouthEast and other emu classes up to and including the Class 455, vehicles for the Docklands Light Railway, and stock for the Strasbourg Eurotram. Later the works became part of British Rail Engineering Limited (BREL) but after the privatisation of BR and having been sold to Asea Brown Bovari Ltd (ABB) closure followed in 1996 with 750 redundancies. A year later, it reopened in the ownership of the American Thrall Car Manufacturing Company for the purpose of wagon construction but after promising early orders from EWS for coal hoppers, flat-bed and ballast wagons, no further work was forthcoming and the factory was finally closed again in 2002 with a further 260 job losses. The main building has now been taken over by Network Rail for the storage and maintenance of Rail Head Treatment Train wagons while other parts of the site have been cleared for housing.

A builder's plate from one of the last batch of Travelling Post Office (TPO) Sorting Vans built at the York Carriage Works. These vehicles, modified Mark 1 coaches, were numbered in the series 80362 to 80374 and though the TPO mail train service ended on 9 January 2004, a number of the ninety-six sorting vans built by BR between 1959 and 1977 have survived into preservation including the last of the York batch, number 80374 built in 1973 and now to be found on the Battlefield Line railway in Leicestershire. Today Royal Mail still moves some ready-sorted letters by rail using Class 325 electric multiple units which pass through York on a regular basis on their journeys between Low Fell on Tyneside and its mail terminal in London (Willesden). The contract for this service is now operated by DB-Cargo.

Not a TPO in which the mail was sorted during the journey, but a Royal Mail electric multiple unit carrying ready-sorted letters. Here on 4 July 2013 Class 325 number 325 006 leads the train out of Holgate Loop into York with 325 016 on the rear.

The west end of York Carriage Works on 13 May 2015 with part of a rail grinder on the 1930s traverser. *Mark 46444*

York Wagon Works was built by the North Eastern Railway in 1867 expanding upon the earlier Queen Street Works of 1842. The 'new' works located near North Junction beside the main line to the north occupied an area of seventeen acres (6.9ha). Its function, like that of the original works, was to carry out locomotive, carriage and wagon repairs, though the job of wagon building, a major occupation in the former works, was to be largely concentrated at sites in Darlington and Shildon after the London and North Eastern Railway (LNER) took over operations at the 'Grouping' of 1923. Following nationalisation under the Transport Act of 1947, British Railways embarked upon a programme of rationalisation and closures of workshops with the result that York Wagon Works was eventually closed by 1964. The site remained in operation after that as first Trainload Freight continued to maintain and repair wagons into the 1980s followed by Thrall Europa from their base at the nearby Holgate Road Carriage Works and then from 2011 Freightliner UK took over the site for vehicle maintenance.

The site of the former York Wagon Works now operated by Freightliner UK as seen on 4 July 2013.

NOT FORGETTING CHOCOLATE

York has long been the home of great chocolate manufacturers with Rowntrees and Terry's being at the forefront of the confectionary trade. Rowntrees' involvement dates back to 1862 with the subsequent development of the Cocoa Works on Haxby Road from 1897. Shortly afterwards, in 1901, nearby land was purchased by the Rowntree family to build New Earswick, a community 'for the improvement of the working classes . . . by the provision of improved dwellings with open spaces', standing in stark opposition to the abject poverty of the working classes living in York's slums. In its heyday 14,000 people were employed by the confectionary companies in York and Rowntrees even instituted a railway passenger train service to its factory for workers commuting in from areas such as Selby or Doncaster. Rowntree Halt station was a minor unmanned stop on the Foss Islands branch of the York to Scarborough line opened by the LNER from Burton Lane Junction in 1927. The single short platform was adjacent to a signal-protected siding which allowed freight direct access to the factory complex. Passenger services to the factory ran until 1988 and the station was officially closed on 8 July 1989. The line itself was demolished in 1992 and part of it is now a cycle track.

Within the Haxby Road factory was 1.5 miles (2.4 km) of standard gauge track operated at first by a second-hand Hudswell Clarke loco named *Marshall* bought in 1890, later to be replaced by an 0-4-0 saddle tank, *Newton*, bought from the Manchester Ship Canal Company in 1895. Further locos were added, including their first 'new' engine named *Locomotive No.2* in 1909, then a third in 1915 and finally a fourth named *Swansea* in 1943, all being used for moving coal and general shunting duties within the factory limits. All four were eventually scrapped on site in 1959 when diesel engines took over.

On 24 August 1981 a dmu waits at Rowntree Halt to take workers to Selby at the end of their shift.

YORK'S OTHER STATION

The Derwent Valley Railway, York, was once a source of considerable traffic for what was known as the 'York Cattle Market branch', later called the Foss Islands Branch, opened in 1879 and departing from the York to Scarborough line at Burton Lane Junction, just over a mile (about 1.8km) from York station. Originally built to serve the then new cattle market to the east of the city, this thriving business was the line's major source of revenue through into the 1960s, along with other traffic including freight of all kinds but especially coal, petrol, bricks, seed potatoes from Scotland and sand for the manufacture of glass bottles at the nearby Redfern National Glass works. The large Rowntree Mackintosh chocolate factory became the largest single source of traffic on the line from the 1970s.

The Foss Islands end of the branch line passing Rowntree's factory connected with the terminus of the Derwent Valley Light Railway (DVLR) at York's 'other station', Layerthorpe, which was opened in 1913. The DVLR was primarily an independent freight line carrying mainly agricultural produce from along its route to Cliffe Common near Selby, with intermediate stations at Osbaldwick, Murton Lane, Dunnington, Elvington, Wheldrake, Cottingwith, Thorganby and Skipwith. It was known locally as the 'Blackberry Line' when it was used to carry the fruit from bramble picking on Skipwith Common to markets in Yorkshire and beyond. A major source of freight was Yorkshire Grain Driers Ltd of Dunnington, which supplied dried barley in bulk for the scotch whisky industry but when this contract was lost the future of the line seemed bleak. An attempt was made in the mid 1970s, to attract passengers back to the line by working with the newly opened National Railway Museum (NRM) to run steam hauled trains from Layerthorpe to Dunnington (4.5 miles, 6.5km). On 9 October 1976 LNWR 'Improved Precedent' Class 2-4-0 number 790 *Hardwicke* attracted considerable interest when she worked a special excursion service between the two stations with three runs in each direction and 300 passengers carried. The event was regarded

Though early indications were encouraging with trains headed by LNWR number 790 *Hardwicke* drawing good numbers of passengers, the slightly 'out of town' location of the line from Layerthorpe to Dunnington proved a step too far for many visitors. Built at Crewe Works in 1892 and on loan from the NRM where she is part of the National Collection of historic rail vehicles, she is seen here at Layerthorpe on 9 October 1976.

as market research into the prospects of operating further steam hauled excursions on a regular basis with traction being provided by LNER Class J72 0-6-0T number 69023 *Joem*, but the venture proved unattractive as a long term project and was abandoned three years later.

Though traffic from the Dunnington Industrial Estate continued into the 1970s; it was the business generated by the Rowntree factory which ensured the commercial survival of the Foss Islands branch until 1989 by which time the company was transferring its distribution to road haulage resulting in the closure of the line. The tracks were lifted in 1992.

Following the trial runs using the NRM's loco *Hardwicke*, subsequent journeys to the end of the line at Dunnington were in the capable hands of Class J72 number 69023 *Joem*, seen here on 7 August 1977. Built at Darlington Works in 1951, she was withdrawn from shed 52A Gateshead in October 1962. Saved into preservation she is now owned by the North Eastern Locomotive Preservation Group and has worked on several heritage lines, most recently the Wensleydale Railway north of York near Northallerton.

Layerthorpe station, 30 August 1979, and it's the 'end of the line' for the Derwent Valley Light Railway on the Foss Islands branch after J72 *Joem* has brought in her train from Dunnington and will be stabled in the tiny one-road shed beyond the station for the final time.

Cast iron weight restriction signs were once a common sight on bridges which carried minor roads over the tracks. This pair adorned the bridge on the approach to Layerthorpe station, seen here on 30 August 1979.

The upper sign reads:

This BRIDGE is insufficient to carry a HEAVY MOTOR CAR the Registered Axle Weight of any axle of which exceeds FIVE TONS or the Registered Axle Weights of the several axles exceeds in the aggregate SEVEN TONS or a Heavy Motor Car drawing a TRAILER if the Registered Axle Weights of the several axles of the Heavy Motor Car and the Axle Weights of the several axles of the TRAILER exceed in aggregate 12 TONS.

NORTH EASTERN RAILWAY CO. YORK.

To further emphasise the point, the lower sign reads:

NORTH EASTERN RAILWAY
NOTICE
THIS BRIDGE IS INSUFFICIENT TO CARRY WEIGHTS BEYOND THE ORDINARY TRAFFIC OF THE DISTRICT. LOCOMOTIVE AND OTHER ENGINES ARE PROHIBITED FROM PASSING OVER IT.
C.N. WILKINSON
SECRETARY

CHAPTER TWO

DIESELS TAKE OVER

The scene at York North mpd on 20 May 1962 as Class A1 number 60140 *Balmoral* rests between turns. She was outshopped from Darlington Works in December 1948 and worked until January 1965 before being withdrawn and scrapped.

DISAPPEARING SIGNAL BOXES

As the age of steam came to an end, so the age of the diesel locomotive transformed our railways, not just in terms of traction but more widely to include the whole infrastructure in and around the station. After the official 'end of steam' in 1968 and the ban on running the few preserved locos on the national network it was widely assumed that the ensuing modernisation would soon sweep away all remnants of the 'old days'. Indeed, familiar facets of the railway scene disappeared over the following years as the relentless march of progress took its toll. The signal box is a case in point. York's extensive rail system was managed by a host of boxes, some in and around the station itself and others along the diverging lines, ranging in size from little more than a crossing keeper's cabin to substantial structures with over a hundred levers. Level crossings, always considered to be danger points on the system, were removed where possible or electrically operated to reduce human error. The heavy and robust cast iron signs and notices which adorned the track-side also vanished – some for scrap but others into collections both official and unofficial.

Marston Moor on the once busy York to Harrogate branch by way of Knaresborough, now reduced to single track between Poppleton and Hammerton, boasted a typical country station with a manually operated level crossing and semaphore signals, as seen here in March 1975. Dating from the 'railway mania' period, the line was built in three stages from 1848 to 1862 initially by the East & West Yorkshire Junction Railway, a company backed by George Hudson, the 'Railway King', who negotiated an agreement whereby it would make a junction with the Great North of England Company and use the station at York. Today the station at Marston Moor is closed, the platforms overgrown and the old heavy wooden gates have been replaced.

On the same line and also not far from York, the station and its crossing at Cattal have fared rather better than some others, as seen here on 9 October 2014.

The crossing box at Cattal still functions to control the passage of trains through the station between York and Knaresborough, as witnessed on 9 October 2014. In spite of the parallel bus route which offers a more frequent service but visits several nearby villages, passenger traffic on the branch is still regular and the route well used because of its much shorter journey time.

The nearest station to York on this interesting old line which still boasts semaphore signals and manually operated crossing gates is Poppleton. Since the closure of Norton South signal box near Stockton on the Durham Coast line in early February 2021, built by the North Eastern Railway in 1870, it is believed that the box at Poppleton shown above and dating from 1871 is now the joint oldest signal box still in use by Network Rail, an honour it shares with boxes at Bootle and Drigg on the Cumbrian Coast Line and Llanfair PG on Anglesey. Seen here on 11 July 2013, the signalman receives the single line token from the crew of WCRC Class 47 number 47 237 which is at the head of The Royal Scotsman on its eight day 'Grand Tour of Great Britain'.

Bootham level crossing to the east of York station on the Scarborough line in April 1976. The box was closed and demolished in 1989 and the crossing fitted with automatic barriers. Rowntree's chocolate factory can be seen in the background.

York Yard North signal box in February 1980. Its 150 levers controlled the goods lines between Holgate Junction and Skelton Junction, though this number was later reduced to just sixty before, like so many others, it became a casualty of the York re-signalling programme of the late 1980s. Its original traditional style roof had to make way for the construction of the new road to Clifton which opened on 28 October 1963. Prior to this the only way across the adjacent River Ouse at Clifton Scope was the Water End Ferry. It cost one penny (1d) to cross the river.

Within the station itself, the former Platform signal box survives as a bookshop and newsagent with the upper storey being converted to a café accessible from the footbridge. It is the only survivor of the four manual signal boxes which once controlled the movements of trains through the station. The large NER clock has been restored with blue dials and gold numerals and finial. Facing passengers as they come across the footbridge is a third smaller dial and below it the City of York Coat of Arms.

Signalling in the York area today is largely managed from York Rail Operating Centre (York ROC), one of twelve which will eventually control all signalling throughout mainland UK. York ROC became operational in January 2015 and is located next to the station on the former Engineers' Triangle, an area previously used to turn steam locomotives. This necessitated the installation of a traditional turntable beside the freight yard. The building will eventually house some 400 signallers, replacing over 1,000 employed across the whole London North Eastern Region and will manage the largest route mileage on the mainland including the whole ECML from King's Cross to the Scottish Borders. The twenty-first century technology employed here is a far cry from that described in the May 1923 *Railway Magazine* where it was noted that a new train control system had recently (November 1922) been introduced at York by the LNER which covered all main line traffic in the area and when fully operational would allow trains to be 'followed' as they progressed between Shaftholme Junction north of Doncaster and Newcastle Central station. It went on to explain how the York system employed a new concept in train diagramming involving a clockwork arrangement using 'carriers' to represent the trains, which are attached to cords when the train enters the control area. The carriers then move along the board, marked with every signal box, station, siding, etc. on this 'endless belt' system at a rate controlled by gears set for each cord (ie. line) according to the scheduled working speed of the various classes of train. By this method, it concluded, 'a visual indication of the approximate position of each train in the control area is afforded at any time'. It was also noted that the controllers at York would be in telephone communication with 'reporting points' such as stations along the route so that adjustments could be made (ie. the carrier repositioned) on the board to take into account the actual progress made by each train. A high-tech innovation at the time!

York's Rail Operating Centre is located next to the station alongside the 'Parcels Sidings' by platform 11. The sidings are frequently used to park locos awaiting their next job. On 11 January 2019, DB Schenker Class 67 number 67 018 *Keith Heller* is seen in the sidings in front of the ROC on 'Thunderbird' duty, ready to be called into service to rescue any train broken down in the area.

THE NATIONAL RAILWAY MUSEUM COMES TO YORK

The Transport Museum at Clapham, London established in 1959 had been open only five years when as part of their Transport Bill the Government revealed their plan to create a branch of the Science Museum to be known as the National Railway Museum and that although several sites throughout the country were under consideration the preferred option was York. The decision was met with considerable opposition, not least from some London Members of Parliament and the resultant argument and counter argument raged for several years as supporters of the Clapham site tried in vain to preserve the status quo. Their case was not a convincing one however, as the Clapham site had always been seen as less than ideal in not having a rail connection or the land available for expansion. In addition, over the previous two years the museum had incurred a considerable financial loss and visitor numbers of 156,000 in 1967 did not compare favourably with, say, the Science Museum where attendance in the same period was almost 2 million per year. As was pointed out at the time, London already had several prestigious museums and indeed the Science Museum itself housed a considerable collection of railway relics. Answering questions in the House of Commons in 1968, the Minister responsible stressed that the entire weight of expert opinion was against the preservation of Clapham as a centre in this respect, going on to explain that York, which is closely associated with early railway history and is a great tourist centre in its own right, would be a most suitable location, adding that the proposed site would have a direct connection into the railway network allowing the easy movement of exhibits into and out of the museum as well as ample room for expansion.

Nevertheless, the Transport Trust, a registered charity founded in 1965 to act as a hub for the transport preservation movement, providing advice and guidance as well as working to secure suitable accommodation and maintenance facilities for historic items, threw its weight behind the objections to move what would become the enlarged National Collection to York, launching an appeal to the Ombudsman after a number of requests for a public enquiry had been turned down by the government. So the argument raged on, not least in the House of Lords where some were outraged by the Government's use of the 'guillotine' procedure on the Transport Bill in the House of Commons which in effect denied time for debating the final clauses including that relating to transport relics. The Transport Act 1968 was eventually passed and a date set for the completion of work on the new building in York, which was to be the second half of 1971. Allowing a year for the movement of exhibits, the National Railway Museum (NRM) was therefore expected to open in 1972.

Occupying the site of the former York North locomotive depot dating back to 1878, delays resulted in the NRM opening its doors to the public on 28 September 1975, having taken the former BR collections from Clapham and the York Railway Museum located at Queen Street. The museum was administered by what was then the Department for Education and Science as an outstation of the Science Museum at South Kensington, London. The official opening on 27 September was timed to coincide with the 150th anniversary of the Stockton & Darlington Railway, with the honours being performed by HRH the Duke of Edinburgh. Part of the Science Museum Group, it boasts over 6,000 objects on display including locomotives and items of rolling stock with many more in storage, making it the largest museum of its kind in Britain. The main display hall (later named The Great Hall) is located in what used to be numbers three and four sheds of York North Depot and exhibits are grouped round two turntables with a track linking them and a connection out of the building to the main line. Generally the locos are grouped around the larger turntable with twenty-four tracks radiating from it, while rolling stock is arranged around the smaller turntable with its twenty tracks. Pits beneath some of the tracks off the main turntable have been modernised and fitted with lighting to show details between the loco frames and one has been deepened to allow visitors to walk beneath the locomotive that stands over it. In addition to locos and rolling stock, the Great Hall also houses exhibits from stationary engine days including the Weatherhill winding engine from the Stanhope & Tyne Railway and the Leicester & Swannington engine as well as a vast collection of items of railway interest both large and small. The emphasis has always been on display and to this end a viewing gallery was incorporated running the full length of the hall. An extensive library and railway research archive have also been added. Its 'outpost', Locomotion – the NRM at Shildon, County Durham, opened in 2004 and is home to further locomotives in the National Collection as well as many other objects detailing the history of railways.

Outside the newly opened National Railway Museum in October 1975 the world's first iron railway bridge was re-erected, having previously been an exhibit in the Queen Street museum. Designed by George Stephenson to carry the Stockton & Darlington Railway (S&D Rly) across the River Gaunless near Shildon, its first three spans were erected in 1823 with a fourth added two years later. Mounted on rails on the bridge is a chauldron wagon, also from the S&D Rly.

Inside the newly opened museum, more than twenty locos formed the centre-piece of the display, many arranged around one of the turntables which occupy what is now the Great Hall. Within the first three weeks, more than 170,000 visitors had flocked through the doors, with the one millionth being welcomed after just seven months.

The National Collection is made up of around 280 rail vehicles of which about 100 are housed at York at any one time with the remainder being housed at Locomotion, Shildon, the Science Museum, Kensington, London, the Science and Industry Museum in Manchester or on loan to other museums and heritage railways. The collection includes vehicles from the earliest wagonways of around 1815 through to such famous locomotives as GNR number 1, the 'Stirling Single' of 1870, LNWR number 790 *Hardwicke* of 1892, GWR number 3440 *City of Truro* from 1903, LNER A3 number 60103 *Flying Scotsman* of 1923, LNER A4 number 4468 *Mallard* of 1938, LMS Princess Coronation Class number 6229 *Duchess of Hamilton* also from 1938 and the last steam locomotive built for BR, 9F number 92220 *Evening Star* of 1960, to name but a few. Also in the collection are a number of narrow gauge, broad gauge, diesel and electric locos and multiple units, not forgetting numerous examples of coaching stock and goods wagons.

The NRM has been at the centre of several major projects over the years including celebrating important railway anniversaries by staging 'RailFest' events, the purchase and maintenance of the iconic *Flying Scotsman* and in 2012 the repatriation of two LNER Class A4 locomotives, numbers 60008 *Dwight D. Eisenhower* and 60010 *Dominion of Canada*. These were to be cosmetically restored and temporarily reunited with their four surviving 'sisters', number 60007 *Sir Nigel Gresley*, 60009 *Union of South Africa*, 4464 *Bittern* and 4468 *Mallard* herself, for 'Mallard 75 - The Great Gathering' held from 3 to 17 July the following year, celebrating the record holder's achievement seventy-five years previously. The event was a great success. The NRM recorded its busiest ever period with 140,000 visitors attending over the two weeks.

The first RailFest held at the NRM was in 2004 to celebrate several important railway anniversaries including 200 years since Richard Trevithick's first railway locomotive and 100 years since *City of Truro*'s high speed run. Seen here at the 2012 RailFest, held to celebrate the theme of 'Record Breakers', GWR 3700 Class number 3440 *City of Truro* works alongside streamlined LMS Coronation Pacific number 6229 *Duchess of Hamilton* on 5 June 2012. Number 3440 is held by many to be the first steam loco to achieve 100mph (161km/h) when it headed its train from Plymouth to London Paddington in 1904, though this 'unofficial' timing has always been contentious as the run by LNER A3 number 4472 *Flying Scotsman* with her test train on 30 November 1934 is acknowledged as the first to officially attain that speed.

More modern traction on show at RailFest 2012 in the shape of Network Rail Windhoff Multi Purpose Vehicle number DR 98973 and in the background GBRf Class 92 electric loco number 92 032 in Europorte livery. These locos were used on international freight traffic duties between the UK and Calais as well as domestic freight and on contract to Caledonian Sleepers to power overnight sleeping car services between Euston and Scotland.

On the same date, 5 June 2012, visitors to RailFest 2012 admire world speed record holder LNER A4 number 4468 *Mallard* which set the bar at 126mph (203km/h) between Grantham and Peterborough on 3 July 1938. Other notable engines on display at the event included Furness Railway number 20, the oldest working standard gauge steam locomotive in the UK, SR Schools Class number 925 *Cheltenham*, GWR Hall Class number 5972 *Olton Hall* (as '*Hogwarts Castle*'), LMS Jubilee number 45596 *Bahamas*, LMS Princess Royal number 6201 *Princess Elizabeth*, LNER *Flying Scotsman* (still undergoing restoration and displayed in black livery as number 502), LNER A4 number 60007 *Sir Nigel Gresley* and 'New Build' A1 number 60163 *Tornado*. Also present to view were a number of 'industrials' and diesel locos representing classes 08, 33, 37, 40, 50, 55, 56 and 57.

Before the crowds come in for 'Mallard 75 – The Great Gathering', the six surviving Gresley A4 Pacifics can be seen arranged around the turntable in the Great Hall of the NRM on 10 July 2013. From the left they are number 60007 *Sir Nigel Gresley*, 60008 *Dwight D. Eisenhower* (on loan from the National Railroad Museum, Green Bay, Wisconsin, USA), 60009 *Union of South Africa*, 4464 *Bittern*, 4468 *Mallard* and 4489 *Dominion of Canada* (on loan from the Canadian Railroad Historical Association). The two North American visitors had been cosmetically restored at the NRM before taking their places in this unique line up and would be returned to their owners upon completion of these celebrations.

As part of the city's annual flagship digital arts and lighting festival, 'Illuminating York', the NRM staged the event 'Locos in a Different Light' in 2014. The theme for the year was 'Leading Lights', uncovering the rich history and future of innovation and discovery in the city of York.

During the event in the NRM, several locos from the National Collection were shown off with dramatic and atmospheric lighting, including GWR 'King' Class number 6000 *King George V* seen here on 30 October 2014.

'SHUNTERS'

Amongst the earliest diesel locomotive introductions were the English Electric 350/400hp 0-6-0 shunters, later widely known as class 08, built at BR's works at Crewe, Derby, Doncaster, Darlington and Horwich from 1952. Originally numbered between 13000 and 13365, later D3000 to D4192 (not all numbers used), they eventually totalled some 996 examples when their production ended in 1962. They were the most numerous of all British locomotive classes and became the general-purpose shunter used throughout the network, whether it be for moving wagons in sidings or goods yards or coaching stock in stations. In fact, wherever a shunting job was required, it would most likely be an 08 which would perform the task. Nothing lasts forever of course and by 1973, when the TOPS reclassification system was introduced re-numbering them from 08 001 through to 08 958, several had already been withdrawn, the first being D3193 in 1967. By 1964 York North shed had an allocation of fifteen 08 shunters amongst its remaining steam locomotives.

Class 08 shunter number 08 245 moves a rake of wagons into York Yard North while a permanent way gang checks the track during August 1979. Over seventy examples from the class have survived into preservation and can be seen at heritage railway sites throughout the country, though unfortunately 08 245 was not one of the lucky ones.

Class 08 number 08 224 trundles through the station during the 1980s.

In York mpd yard in August 1988 are Class 08 shunters numbers 08 500 *Thomas* and 08 771. Number 08 500 was built in April 1958, withdrawn in September 1983 only to be reinstated in November 1984. She is now in store, owned by the 'spot-hire' company Harry Needle Railroad, based at Barrow Hill Engine Shed in Derbyshire. Number 08 771 was built in March 1960, withdrawn in March 1992 and scrapped by Gwent Demolition (Margam) in September 1994.

In addition to its Class 08 diesel electric locomotives, York North shed in the mid-1960s was home to fifteen Class 03 and four Class 04 0-6-0 diesel mechanical shunters. Here 03 089 is working at Holgate sidings just to the west of the station on 2 July 1984. She was one of the 230 such locos built at Doncaster and Swindon Works and introduced from 1957. As with the 08 design, many have been saved into preservation including 03 089 which is operational at the Mangapps Railway Museum, a heritage railway centre near Burnham-on-Crouch, Essex.

DIESEL MULTIPLE UNITS

In the aftermath of the nationalisation of the railways and the subsequent 1955 'Modernisation Plan' a large fleet of diesel multiple units (dmus) were built in BR's own workshops and by numerous private contractors. By the early 1980s these 'First Generation' dmus, built between 1956 and 1963 and allocated to TOPS Classes 100 to 131, were nearing the end of their design life. This led to BR embarking upon its so-called 'Sprinterisation' programme which produced the 'Second Generation' Classes 140 to 144 'Pacer' railbuses – diesel mechanical four-wheeled vehicles for provincial lines, and the 'Sprinter' family of diesel hydraulic multiple units which comprised Class 150 'Sprinters' for branch line and commuter trains, Class 153/155/156 'Super Sprinters' for longer cross-country services and Class 158/159 'Express Sprinters' for secondary express services, as well as the Class 165 and 166 'Network Turbo' and 'Network Express' diesel hydraulic units aimed specifically at the non-electric commuter services into London. The vast majority of these 'Second Generation' dmu sets are still in service and many can be seen regularly in York.

Above: Built by the Gloucester Railway Carriage and Wagon Company in 1957 and previously numbered 56101 and 51116, this Class 100 dmu set seen at York on 24 February 1983 was given a further lease of life after being withdrawn from Norwich depot on 28 October 1972 and transferred into departmental stock to become Civil Engineers' Department 'Manager's Saloon' numbers DB 975539 and DB 975349. Sporting its 'York Saloon' headboard, the unit was based at York depot for a time but eventually was withdrawn from Cambridge depot in January 1993 to be scrapped at MC Metals, Glasgow in August of that year.

Opposite below: Thirty Class 110 dmu sets were built by the Birmingham Carriage & Wagon Company between 1961 and 1962 and many worked in the Yorkshire area. These were the penultimate class of 'First Generation' dmus and most sets were based at Bradford Hammerton Street depot until this closed in 1984 when they were transferred to Leeds Neville Hill. Usually seen working as two-car units comprising a Driving Motor Brake Composite (DMBC) and a Driving Motor Composite Lavatory (DMCL) especially after their refurbishment in 1979 to 1980 when many Trailer Standard Lavatory (TSL) coaches were removed, most had been scrapped by 1991. One of the two surviving sets is seen above working near York on the Wensleydale Railway on 4 March 2012. Restored to BR Green livery DMBC number E51813 and DMCL number E51842 wait at Leyburn station with their train for Leeming Bar.

BR Metropolitan Cammell Class 101 dmu set S800 comprising cars 51445 and 51495 waits at the platform after bringing in a train from Sheffield to York in August 1988. Number 51445 was built in May 1959 and allocated first to depot 62A Thornton Junction. Withdrawn in February 1993 she was subsequently scrapped at M.C. Metal Processing, Springburn, Glasgow. Number 51495 was built in February 1959 and allocated to 51A Darlington depot. She was withdrawn from Leeds Neville Hill depot in the same year and scrapped by Mayer Newman at Snailton, Cambridgeshire.

'Pacers'

The dmu classes 140 to 144 were known as 'Pacers'. They were constructed between 1980 and 1987 and numbered 165 sets in total, their design being based on the Leyland 'National' bus producing a lightweight modified bus body carried on a long wheel-base four-wheel freight wagon type underframe. The aim was to replace the ageing 'first generation' dmus with a fleet of rail-buses which were economical to build and inexpensive to operate, with a life expectancy of not more than twenty years. However due to delays in the production and introduction of replacement rolling stock over forty sets were still operational in 2020, many in the York area which by this time were over thirty-five years old. With the introduction by Northern Trains Limited (the publicly owned successor to Northern Rail and later Arriva Rail North) of their Class 195 CAF 'Civity' units from 2019, refurbished 'Sprinters' have been released to replace 'Pacers' on certain routes.

Northern Rail Class 142 'Pacer' set 142 004 approaches Colton Junction, York on 14 July 2015 with 2C18, a Leeds to York service. The largest 'Pacer' class, ninety-six units were introduced from 1985, built by BREL in cooperation with the Leyland Bus Company, comprising an Aluminium body and roof on a steel underframe. They were numbered 142 001 to 142 096. Though many were scrapped or retired into storage, being replaced by 'Sprinters', a number have been returned to service coupled to Class 150s during the 2020 Covid-19 pandemic to provide extra capacity and 'social distancing'. Fifteen units have been preserved.

Northern Rail Class 144 'Pacer' set 144 003 heads away from York at Colton Junction on 9 April 2013 with a service to Sheffield. Twenty-three units were built by BREL in cooperation with Walker Alexander Coachbuilders of Falkirk and introduced from 1986. They continued in service until 2020, mainly in the South Yorkshire area for Northern Trains in spite of their not meeting new disability regulations relating to wheel-chair access. However when rail services were reduced due to the Covid-19 pandemic they were stored out of use at Keighley on the Keighley & Worth Valley Railway and at Heaton TMD. Eight units have been preserved.

'Sprinters'

The 'Sprinter' family of dmus, Classes 150 to 159, were introduced into service from 1984, 556 sets being built into the early 1990s by BREL, Metro Cammell and Leyland and put to work by Train Operating Companies throughout Great Britain from Abellio ScotRail to the South Western Railway. In the York area they were operated by Northern Rail, later Northern Trains.

Northern Rail Class 150 'Sprinter' set number 150 119 at Bolton Percy between York and Leeds with train 2R95 York to Hull service on 17 December 2016. The 134 Class 150 sets were built as 2-car units with five-abreast seating and no end gangway, so when coupled with other units for multiple working the passengers were not able to move between units. Later versions featured two-by-two airline type seating and end gangways.

Former GWR Class 150 'Sprinter' set number 150 123 approaching Colton Junction on 3 May 2018 with train 2R84 from Hull to York. One of a batch recently displaced from the West Country upon the introduction of emus.

Northern Rail Class 153 'Super Sprinter' number 153 330 at Colton with 2Y80, a Sheffield to York service on 16 June 2015. The 'Super Sprinters' are single-car units converted from the earlier Class 155 two-car sets during 1991 and 1992, being intended for operation on lightly used lines. Seventy cars were produced.

Northern Rail Class 153 'Super Sprinter' number 153 363 waits at the platform at York station ready to take a service to Sheffield on 30 June 2015.

Class 155 'Super Sprinter' number 155 345 waits at York to take her train to Liverpool Lime Street during October 1989. Sporting the original carmine and cream Metro Train livery she was built in 1988 by Leyland Bus at Workington, one of forty-two such sets. Only seven are still in service, numbers 155 341 to 155 347, the remaining thirty-five having been converted to Class 153 single coach rail-cars. Built for the West Yorkshire Passenger Transport Executive for use on their Metro Train routes, they are now operated by Northern Trains and most frequently seen on Manchester Victoria to Leeds services.

Northern Rail Class 158 'Express Sprinter' set number 158 906 in special 'advertising York' livery leaving Colton Junction on 30 June 2015 with train 1B18, a York to Blackpool North service. The 'Express Sprinters' are the largest class in the Sprinter family with a total of 182 units being produced, mainly as two-car sets. Built from 1989 to 1992 by BREL at Derby's Litchurch Lane Works they were described by BR at the time as 'bringing new standards of comfort and quality to rail travel on the Regional Railways' key long-distance cross-country routes', having 'panoramic' windows, full carpeting, airline-style seats with tables, air conditioning and provision of a refreshment trolley service. In the York area they continue to be operated by Northern Trains which acquired additional units from Abellio ScotRail and First TransPennine Express.

Northern Rail Class 158 'Express Sprinter' set number 158 849, outshopped in 'Tour de France' livery, stands at York station on 16 October 2014 waiting to take train 1B20 to Blackpool North.

'Turbostars'

The Class 170 'Turbostar' class of dmus were built by Bombardier Transportation at Derby between 1998 and 2005, during which time a total of 139 units were produced. Most are owned by Porterbrook and a few (numbers 170 416 to 170 424) belong to the Eversholt Rail Group and are leased to the Train Operating Companies. They were built with the intention of replacing the remaining 'Pacers' as well as the 'Sprinters' and the now aged Class 205 and 207 diesel electric multiple units which had been built during the 1950s and 1960s for the Southern Region of BR. Abellio ScotRail is the largest operator of Class 170s and from 2018 sixteen units were transferred to Arriva Rail North, then from March 2020 on to Northern Trains. These units, built in 2004 and 2005, are maintained at Leeds Neville Hill and Hull Botanic Gardens depots, numbered 170 453 to 170 461 and 170 472 to 170 478, and in the York area can be seen operating around the Harrogate Loop.

Following the privatisation of BR in the late 1990s, further diesel hydraulic dmu families have appeared in the York area including most notably the Class 185 'Desiro' units built by Siemens and introduced by First TransPennine Express. Later Northern Trains would introduce the Class 195 'Civity' sets on its non-electrified routes while on long distance services Cross Country's Class 220/221 'Voyager' and 'Super Voyager' sets would dominate. The long-distance rail route known as the Cross-Country Route superseded the Midland Railway in its central section and runs from Bristol to York via Birmingham, Derby, Sheffield and Leeds. The East Midland Railway (EMR) 'Meridian' Class 222 fleet also occasionally ventures as far as York.

Northern Trains Class 170 'Turbostar' set number 170 475 at York station on 10 September 2020 waiting to take 2C49, a York to Leeds via Harrogate service.

'Desiros'

The fifty-one sets of Class 185 'Desiro' dmus built by Siemens in Germany between 2005 and 2008 were intended to replace Class 158 and 175 sets. These new units were required, under the terms of the franchise agreement, to be capable of 100mph (161km/h) running, feature air conditioning, additional toilet facilities, wheelchair access, bicycle storage space and other improvements over existing stock. Designed for use on hilly routes, they would become a familiar sight on services between Manchester, Yorkshire and the North East of England. Also specified in the agreement was the construction of maintenance and stabling facilities, with the main depot being at Ardwick, Manchester and a second at Leeman Road, York which opened in May 2007. A refurbishment programme started in May 2017 saw the inclusion of new seating and improved decor, refitted toilets, LED lighting and USB and standard plug sockets at every pair of seats.

First TransPennine Express Class 185 'Desiro' set number 185 151 passes Towthorpe on 8 September 2016 having just left York as 1E83 Liverpool Lime Street to Scarborough.

Class 185 'Desiro' set number185 123 passes Colton on 20 July 2016 in First TransPennine Express 'new livery' with 1P33 York to Manchester Airport service.

Northern Trains Class 195 CAF 'Civity' number 195 003 at the platform at York with 2T20 York to Leeds on 10 September 2020. The fifty-eight units built by the Spanish company CAF and owned by Eversholt Rail Group are currently operated by Northern Trains from 2019. The stated aim at their introduction was for a 'step change in quality' compared with their now less than popular predecessors the 'Pacers' and 'Sprinters'.

Cross Country Class 220 'Voyager' set led by 220 008 at York station on 10 September 2020 with 1V62 Newcastle to Bristol Temple Meads. The Class 220 'Voyager' diesel-electric high-speed multiple units were built by Bombardier in Belgium in 2000 and 2001 for the Cross-Country Route and are capable of 125mph (200km/h) running. The thirty-four trains operate as four-coach sets often in multiple with the similar Class 221 'Super Voyagers' and were intended to replace the long-lived Class 47 locomotives with their Mark 2 carriages as well as the Inter City 125 sets.

Cross Country Class 221 'Super Voyager' set led by 221 133 at Bolton Percy on 31 August 2012. The Class are often used in multiple with the four-car Class 220 'Voyager' sets.

EMR Class 222 'Meridian' set led by 222 006 at York station with 1F01 Leicester to York on 15 December 2019. Built by Bombardier in Belgium from 2003 they are similar to the Class 220 'Voyager' and Class 221 'Super Voyager' trains but with a different interior. They are operated today by East Midlands Railway whose services include trains from London St. Pancras along the Midland Main Line to Nottingham and Sheffield with limited extensions to Lincoln, Leeds and York.

MAIN LINE DIESEL LOCOMOTIVES

Class 20

As the diesel era progressed, an impressive range of freight as well as passenger locomotives were manufactured to fill the void left by the wholesale removal of steam traction. Several early introductions proved unreliable and were quickly replaced by improved designs, a successful case in point being the BR Class 20, a diesel electric loco also known as the English Electric Type 1. Intended for light freight duties, a total of 228 examples were built at Vulcan Foundry and Robert Stephenson & Hawthorns between 1957 and 1968, being originally numbered D8000 to D8199 and D8300 to D8327. Capable of working 'nose to nose' in multiple, their value was extended and with it their life expectancy as in this formation they could handle heavier traffic at a time when lighter loads were being transferred to road haulage. They were also occasionally used on passenger workings for which a small number were fitted with steam heating equipment. In later years pairs of Class 20s were regularly seen operating Rail Head Treatment Trains (RHTTs) which produced high power water jets containing 'sandite', a material to clean and coat the rails to aid traction, for example during the autumn 'leaf-fall' period.

From 1976, most of the class were withdrawn, though since rail privatisation some twenty-three are main-line registered to continue to operate over the network and a further twenty have been preserved including class-leader D8000 (TOPS number 20 050) which is now part of the National Collection based at the NRM, York.

BR Class 20s numbers 20 201 and 20 054 work a partially fitted freight down the ECML north of York near Beningbrough on 12 August 1975.

Approaching Colton Junction to the west of York on 12 October 2012 a pair of Direct Rail Services (DRS) Class 20s operate a Rail Head Treatment Train. Leading is number 20 301 with 20 302 at the rear. In more recent times these workings have been taken by pairs of Class 66 locos.

Painted in the maroon livery of the Metropolitan Line of the London Underground network, Class 20 number 20 142 *Sir John Betjeman* makes an appearance at York on the rear of 1Z18, the Vintage Trains rail-tour 'The White Rose' on 27 July 2019. The train from Dorridge (Solihull) to York was headed by former LMS Jubilee number 45596 *Bahamas*.

Class 31

In the same year that the Class 20 was making its debut, another successful design was entering the rapidly changing railway scene in the form of BR's Class 31 or Brush Type 2. Numbered from D5500 to D5699 and D5800 to D5862, these 263 locos were to replace steam power on both freight and passenger workings, with many examples being allocated to depots in the Yorkshire region including York, Holbeck and Tinsley. Like the Class 20s their withdrawal began in the mid-1970s and by 2017 none were operational on the network following the last run of Network Rail's 31 233 on a test train in March of that year. Like the Class 20s, their popularity has resulted in some twenty-six having been saved into preservation to run on heritage railways throughout the country including in the York area number 31 119 (D5537) at the Embsay & Bolton Abbey Steam Railway and number 31 454 (D5654) on the Wensleydale Railway. In addition, the first built, number D5500 (TOPS number 31 018), is now part of the National Collection at York.

Class 31/1 number 31 294 approaches York from the north passing Clifton Sidings with a parcels train on 22 August 1979.

In the 1980s Class 31 number 31 209 negotiates the cross-over at Holgate to take the station avoiding line with her train of empties.

Hurrying north from York along the ECML near Overton on 6 May 1986 are a pair of Class 31/1s led by number 31 284.

Preserved class leader number 31 018 featured in the NRM's 'Locos in a Different Light' evening on 30 October 2014, part of the annual 'Illuminating York' event.

Class 37

Between 1960 and 1965, a total of 309 diesel electric locos of BR Class 37, or English Electric Type 3, were built at Vulcan Foundry and Robert Stephenson & Hawthorns. These general-purpose locos initially saw service on BR's Eastern Region but were soon to be found throughout the network. Nicknamed 'Tractors' due to the distinctive sound of their engines, they became a major part of the British Rail Modernisation Plan which saw the replacement of steam by diesel traction. Originally numbered in two series from D6600 to D6608 and from D6700 to D6999 they were later renumbered from 37 001 under the TOPS system and became a regular sight at the head of passenger services and heavy goods trains.

When by the 1980s many Type 2 and Type 3 locos had been withdrawn, the Class 37s became the standard Type 3 design and were maintained accordingly, with many examples still operational to this day. They are in regular use by rail-freight companies including Colas Rail, Direct Rail Services (DRS) and Locomotive Services Limited (LSL). Network Rail (NR) operates its own small fleet for Departmental purposes and the hire company and charter train operator the West Coast Railway Company (WCRC) also maintains a number of main-line registered examples.

Class 37 number 37 083 threads her train through York station on 21 February 1975.

A pair of Class 37s bring their train towards York Yard North at Clifton during the late 1980s. The leading loco is number 37 062 which carried the name *British Steel Corby* between September 1985 and March 1989, coupled with number 37 078, named *Teesside Steelmaster* from May 1984 until June 1996.

Heading north from York during the 1980s are 37 072 and 37 015 having bypassed the station on the 'York Avoider'.

Originally number D6884, Class 37 number 37 184 approaches York at Holgate with a car transporter train in the late 1980s. *Douglas Todd*

Class 37 number 37 505 (D6728) *British Steel Workington* in BR Railfreight Large Logo Grey livery waits at York mpd in the late 1980s. *Douglas Todd*

Having proved to be a popular and reliable design, it is no surprise that so many have been saved into preservation with well over thirty to be found up and down the land including the first of the class to be built, number D6700 (now 37 350), at the NRM York as part of the National Collection.

Following their snow clearing duties, DRS Class 37s numbers 37 218 and 37 608 are parked at York station on 31 January 2013.

Heading an altogether more prestigious working, DRS Class 37s numbers 37 609 and 37 603 double head 1Z83, Compass Tours' 'The Pennine and North Eastern Explorer' charter from Milton Keynes to Durham and return, accelerating away from York on 24 July 2013.

Having brought her engineers' train from Derby Railway Technical Centre (RTC) into York's Holgate sidings on 23 May 2014, Network Rail 97 301 awaits her next duty. Rebuilt from Class 37 number 37 100 she is one of four locos similarly converted and used as test beds for European Rail Traffic Management Systems on the Cambrian route. Sporting NR's yellow livery they are for engineering and departmental train use.

West Coast Railway Company's Class 37s numbers 37 516 *Loch Laidon* and 37 669 in the company's maroon livery run through York station on 11 August 2016 heading for the NRM after bringing the Scarborough Spa Express from Carnforth to Holgate sidings. Stanier 8F number 48151 would take over for the return run to Scarborough.

Class 40

Once the pride of the BR diesel fleet, the English Electric Type 4, later Class 40, diesel electric locomotives were built between 1958 and 1962. Numbered D200 to D399, the 200 examples mainly originated from Vulcan Foundry though a small number (twenty) were built at Robert Stephenson & Hawthorns in Darlington. Such was the pace of diesel locomotive development at the time that they were soon relegated from express passenger workings by more powerful machines but were equally at home heading ordinary passenger services and freight trains, where they proved to be reliable workhorses into the mid-1980s. In their early days they were mainly to be seen on the London Midland Region but could also be encountered on the East Coast Route where they operated out of Gateshead, Thornaby, York and Healey Mills depots.

Originally known as English Electric Type 4s the first ten were considered 'prototypes' and underwent trials mainly over the Great Eastern and East Coast Main Lines. Their success resulted in a further 190 being ordered, with those in the number range D210 to D235 being named after ships operated by the Cunard Line, Elder Dempster Lines and Canadian Pacific Steamships, whose home port of Liverpool was a frequent destination for their trains. However, by about 1970 the Class 40s were no longer working this route and the nameplates were gradually removed.

From 1973 they were renumbered under the TOPS system from 40 001 to 40 199. As all classes in this system had to begin with loco **001 the first of the class, D200, was renumbered to 40 122, a number made vacant by the demise of D322, scrapped following accident damage. By this time Class 40s stabled in the north east were housed at Healey Mills (32 locos), York (21) and Gateshead (8). The first class-members were withdrawn from service in 1976 (numbers 40 005, 40 039 and 40 102) and by 1984 only sixteen were still running, including 40 122 which had been withdrawn, then reinstated to haul enthusiast specials having been out-shopped in its original green livery. With the exception of this loco, the last passenger train hauled by a Class 40 in service was a Birmingham New Street to York train taken by number 40 012 on 27 January 1985. It and fellow survivors were withdrawn the next day, apart from D200/40 122 which continued to run and was later preserved as part of the National Collection in the NRM, York. Seven other Class 40s are preserved, three of which were former Departmental Locomotives numbers 97 406 (40 135), 97 407 (40 012) and 97 408 (40 118). They were among four temporarily returned to service in 1985 to be engaged in the remodelling of the lines around Crewe station and afterwards used on ballast, freight and occasional parcels trains before being finally withdrawn in 1986/87. Only one, number 97 405 (formerly 40 060), was then scrapped, in 1988.

The nameplate carried by Class 40 number D213 from June 1962. As number 40 013 she was withdrawn in 1984 but preserved. Now operational in BR Green livery and main-line registered as part of Locomotive Services Limited's main line diesel fleet housed at Crewe TMD.

Class 40 number 216 *Campania*, later to be number 40 016, rests between shifts outside York depot c.1969. Built during July 1959 she received her nameplates in May 1962 and worked until 1981 when she was withdrawn from service and subsequently scrapped.

Taking water at York station on 21 February 1975 is Class 40 number 40 056 with a Liverpool Lime Street to Newcastle passenger service.

Heading along the ECML north of York near Shipton by Beningbrough with a train of coal empties for Tyne Dock on 21 July 1975 is Class 40 number 40 164.

Class 40 number 40 150 approaches the station passing Holgate platform on 12 April 1982 with a train of ICI agricultural chemical flasks. She would be one of the last sixteen class members, surviving until January 1985.

Under the impressive train shed roof of York station on 9 July 1979 Class 40 number 40 153 takes the centre road with her south bound parcels train.

Class 40 number 40 058 eases away from a signal check on the ECML just north of York at Overton with her train of Ribble Cement trucks on 25 April 1984.

Now running in preservation, Class 40 number D213 (40 013) *Andania* passes Towthorpe to the east of York with 1Z13, the Locomotive Services Limited (LSL) charter 'The Yorkshire Coast Merrymaker' from Crewe to Scarborough and return on 6 October 2018. Tour operator LSL was certified for main line operation in August 2017, mainly working from Crewe station.

Classes 44, 45 and 46

The Sulzer Type 4 diesel electric locomotives were built at BR's Derby Works in 1959 and 1960 and became Class 44. Only ten were built and named after British mountains which led to their becoming known as 'Peaks'. Originally numbered from D1 to D10 and later under TOPS 44 001 to 44 010 they were at the forefront of the race to replace steam traction during BR's modernisation project, being allocated to Camden mpd to work mainly over the West Coast Main Line (WCML). They were soon followed by 127 Class 45 locos, built between 1960 and 1962 and first numbered from D11 to D137 (later 45 001 to 45 077 and from 45 101 to 45 150) and then between 1961 and 1963 by fifty-six making up Class 46, numbered D138 to D193 (46 001 to 46 056). During this time, the ten 'original Peaks' were transferred to Toton, which would become one of the largest diesel depots in the UK. With the electrification of the WCML and the increasing availability of the second and third generation 'Peaks', the Class 44s were regularly relegated to freight duties mainly in the East Midlands area until the entire class of ten was withdrawn between 1976 and 1980. Two have survived into preservation, number D4/44 004 *Great Gable* based at the Midland Railway Centre, Butterley and D8/44 008 *Penyghent* located at Peak Rail, Matlock, both in Derbyshire. The rest were scrapped at Derby Works.

On a rare visit in August 1969, Peak Class 44 number D1 *Scafell Pike* rests between turns at York mpd. Withdrawn in October 1976 she was scrapped in February 1977.

Passing the site of the former station at Copmanthorpe to the west of York on 7 April 1979 with her train to Sheffield is Class 45 number 45 032. Unlike their predecessors the Class 44s, these were regular visitors to York often in charge of trans-Pennine services between Newcastle or Scarborough and Manchester Victoria or Liverpool Lime Street. A sizeable proportion of their number were allocated to Leeds Holbeck depot with a few at Cricklewood and the majority at Toton.

The summer sunshine of August 1979 lifts the scene at York mpd as Class 45 number 45 048 *The Royal Marines* stands alongside Class 37 number 37 019. A further twenty-five class members were named, those being after British Army regiments.

The nameplate and regimental crest carried by Class 45 number 45 014 *The Cheshire Regiment* as she waits at York on 21 February 1975.

The Class 45s became a familiar sight on the Midland Main Line out of London St. Pancras to Nottingham, Sheffield and northwards, which they dominated until the early 1980s when they were displaced by High Speed Trains (HSTs). They continued to perform admirably with services over the Pennines from Liverpool to York and beyond until their withdrawal, which for most occurred between 1985 and 1988, though two locos were still operational into 1989. Number 45 106 was finally withdrawn after catching fire on 3 February 1989, having been initially taken out of service in July 1988 only to be reinstated in August of that year and had headed the Inter City Thames-Eden rail-tour over the demanding Settle & Carlisle route from Leeds just a fortnight earlier. Similarly, number 45 128 reappeared at Tinsley Traction Maintenance Depot in February 1989 following her withdrawal in August 1988, the intention being to carry out the necessary repairs in preparation for her to head two further rail-tours scheduled for Class 45 haulage following the demise of 45 106. However, the work was never completed and she was again withdrawn in April 1989 and sold for scrap, except for her cabs which have been preserved.

Eleven of the class did survive into preservation and one, number D61/45 112 *Royal Army Ordnance Corps*, is registered as main-line operational. A twelfth, number 45 015, has been in store since 1986 and has latterly deteriorated to a derelict condition at the Battlefield Line Railway in Leicestershire and is likely to be sold for scrap.

The final version of the Peak design, designated Class 46, began to appear from Derby Works in 1961 and a total of fifty-six locos would be outshopped over the following two years. Only one member of the class was named, number D163, later to become 46 026, carried that distinction as *Leicestershire and Derbyshire Yeomanry*. They would feature mainly at the head of cross-country passenger services, both north-east-south-west and trans-Pennine as well as being used regularly on long distance freight trains, so were therefore regular visitors to York. The first of the class was withdrawn in 1977 and by the end of 1984 all had been taken out of service, with just three lucky ones surviving into preservation. One unfortunate loco, number 46 009, was given the dubious honour of demonstrating the safety of carrying nuclear waste by rail when on 17 July 1984 in a demonstration organised by the CEGB she was crashed at 100mph (161km/h) into a deliberately derailed wagon carrying a nuclear waste flask on the Old Dalby Test Track near Melton Mowbray in Leicestershire. The event was widely screened on national television and though the locomotive was severely wrecked and was later scrapped on site, the flask suffered barely a scratch and was later put on display to the public outside the NRM York.

On display outside the NRM York on 22 October 1984 is the undamaged nuclear waste flask involved in the demonstration crash with Peak number 46 009 earlier in the year. Behind can be seen the remains of its 'Flatrol' wagon.

Bringing her train into York station on 9 February 1967 is BR Type 4 Peak Class number D184, built at Derby Works during October 1962 and which would later become number 46 047.

Going off duty after bringing in her train, Peak Class 46 number 46 035 moves into the sidings outside what was York Diesel Depot, which closed in January 1982 but whose tracks were still being used for stabling on 17 July 1984.

One of the lucky three. Peak Class 46 number D182/46 045 still earning her keep not far from York on the North Yorkshire Moors Railway on 11 May 2008. On loan for their annual Spring Diesel Gala from the Midland Railway Centre at Butterley where sister loco 46 035 is also based, her other surviving class-mate number 46 010 resides at the Great Central Railway, Nottingham.

Class 47

The 'Brush Type 4' or BR Class 47 diesel electric locomotives built by Brush Traction at BR's Crewe Works and Brush's Falcon Works at Loughborough between 1962 and 1968 eventually would number 512 examples making them the most numerous class of British main-line diesel locomotive. Crewe would produce 202 with Loughborough building 310 of the total, which would see service at the head of express passenger trains throughout the network, being one of the major designs responsible for the ousting of steam locos from these services. They were allocated to depots from Bristol Bath Road to Gateshead, including a handful to York, and continued to give reliable service well into the 1980s, by which time only five had been withdrawn and these as a result of serious accident damage. Originally numbered from D1500 to D1999 with the remaining twelve from D1100 to D1111 they were later reclassified under the TOPS system in batches within the range 47 001 to 47 981. The 'naming' of locomotives had gone out of favour following a ban by the British Railways Board in the late 1960s by which time fewer than twenty Class 47s carried a name, the first being D1666 named *Odin* at Cardiff Canton depot on 12 March 1965. Many were pleased when the tradition was revived and more of the class would receive such an adornment, beginning with 47 460 as *Great Eastern* in 1978, the name-plate being made of car registration plate letters on a black-painted wooden panel and applied at Stratford depot. This temporary name-plate was removed a few weeks later and an official cast alloy version of the same name was applied to 47 169. In total 446 different names have been used, carried by 442 different Class 47 locos.

During the 1990s, the rate of withdrawal of the Class 47s increased as more reached the end of their working lives and new locomotives were introduced, though they remained in demand such that by 2020, fifty-eight years after their introduction, twenty-four examples are still operational on the national network; a further ten fitted with the systems necessary to be main-line registered are in store. Companies operating these include Locomotive Services Limited, Rail Operations Group, Nemesis Rail, Harry Needle Railroad Company and GB Railfreight. Another thirty-three were rebuilt and reclassified to Class 57, their main user being Direct Rail Services with seventeen examples. Thirty-two more Class 47s are in preservation, a number of which are maintained to main-line standard, the largest operator being West Coast Railways with twenty-two examples, ten of which are currently operational and supplemented by eight Class 57s.

Above left: An early example of a name carried by a Class 47 was on 47 083. One of the 'basic' or 47/0 sub-class originally equipped with steam heating, *Orion* is seen at York station on 21 February 1975.

Above right: The nameplate on Class 47 number 47 705. *Douglas Todd*

Class 47 number 47 508 *Great Britain* pauses at York with her train to Scotland in January 1981.

A Class 47 passes under the 'iron bridge' at Holgate to enter York station with an express for Scotland in 1985. Carrying the 'Large Logo' introduced by BR in 1978 and first used on Class 56 freight locos, later extended to Class 37s, 47s and 50s, number 47 467 also carries the 'Highland Rail' logo and snow plough. *Douglas Todd*

Class 47 number 47 477 leaves York passing Holgate with her freight train in the mid-1980s. *Douglas Todd*

Such is the longevity of the Class 47s that to this day a number regularly appear on main-line trains and are frequent visitors to York. Not only are they often used by charter rail operators such as West Coast Railways, but their reliability has seen them given charge of long distance 'prestige' rail-tours including the Northern Belle and even the ultimate in duties, the Royal Train.

The early morning sun lights Class 47 number 47 832 *Solway Princess* as she heads the Northern Belle away from York on 14 October 2011, passing Shipton by Beningbrough. Built at BR Crewe Works and introduced into traffic on 13 August 1964 as number D1610, later to become 47 031, then 47 560 and be named *Tamar*, she retained the name when renumbered again to 47 832 on 19 June 1989. On 11 September 2005, she was renamed *Driver Tom Clark OBE* at Crewe Works Open Day, only to be renamed again at Crewe Gresty Bridge Open Day on 19 July 2008 when she became *Solway Princess*. She is seen above running in the DRS Northern Belle livery with train 1Z90, from Leeds to Edinburgh and return.

Preserved ex Royal Train loco number 47 798 *Prince William* races north from York passing Shipton by Beningbrough with a shuttle between the NRM's York and Shildon museums on 18 September 2011. Another Crewe built loco, this one entering service on 1 February 1965 as number D1656, to become 47 072 from January 1974 and 47 609 from April 1984, then being named *Fire Fly* in August 1985. The name was retained when she was renumbered to 47 834 in July 1989, but the plates were removed in March 1995, prior to being again renumbered to 47 798 and renamed *Prince William*. The loco, which was preserved from August 2004, is based at the NRM, York and carries the 'ER' crest and 'Royal Livery'.

Passing Colton Junction on the southern outskirts of York is preserved Class 47 number 47 580 *County of Essex* on 19 May 2016 with the returning Steam Dreams rail-tour 'The Cathedrals Express', King's Cross to York and return. The return should have been taken by Gresley A3 number 60103 *Flying Scotsman*, but this had been failed with a broken injector. Number 47 580 is owned and operated by the Stratford 47 Group.

Class 50

Built by English Electric at Vulcan Foundry between 1967 and 1968 the fifty Class 50 express passenger locos were initially leased to BR by the manufacturers for ten years for the purpose of working Anglo-Scottish services on the not yet electrified WCML north from Crewe, often operating as a pair of locos. They were numbered D400 to D449, though later became Class 50 numbers 50 001 to 50 049 under TOPS from 1973 and in the 1970s they were all named by BR after Royal Navy ships. The first so honoured was 50 035 named *Ark Royal* by the captain and crew of the aircraft carrier HMS *Ark Royal* in January 1978. With the electrification of the northern section of the WCML in 1974 they were transferred to the Western Region, but following a long period plagued by reliability issues the fleet was refurbished at Doncaster Works between 1979 and 1984 as by this time the leasing arrangement had ended, and BR had completed their purchase from English Electric. It was during this period that examples might be seen in the York area on 'running in' turns between Doncaster and Newcastle.

Proving popular with enthusiasts amongst whom they are known as 'hoovers' on account of their distinctive engine noise, eighteen have been saved into preservation to continue life on our heritage railways, with several being registered for main line running.

Approaching York past the British Sugar Corporation sidings at Clifton during August 1979 is Class 50 number 50 007 *Hercules* with a returning 'running in' turn from Newcastle to Doncaster Works. One of the lucky survivors, number 50 007 is now owned and operated by the Class 50 Alliance, having been withdrawn from service in 1991, reinstated for rail-tour use a year later (renamed as *Sir Edward Elgar*) and later renamed back to *Hercules* in 2014.

Passing Shipton by Beningbrough on the outskirts of York on 19 August 2017 is preserved Class 50 number 50 008 *Thunderer* heading train 5Z50, an empty coaching stock move from Derby to Bishop Auckland. Owned by Garcia Hanson she is based at the site of the freight company Devon & Cornwall Railways (DCR) at Washwood Heath, Birmingham.

Heading north from York on 30 November 2019 a pair of preserved Class 50s now sporting GBRf livery pass Overton with 1Z30, Bristol Temple Meads to Newcastle and return 'The Festive York and Durham Explorer' charter. Leading is number 50 049 *Defiance* accompanied by number 50 014 *Warspite*.

Class 55

Vulcan Foundry was again at the forefront of diesel traction building when during 1961 and 1962 English Electric produced twenty-two express passenger locomotives with engines unlike any used on the railways before. These were the production 'Deltics', so named because of the arrangement of their cylinders in three blocks forming a triangle reminiscent of the Greek letter delta. They were conceived and built with one purpose in mind, to replace fifty-five 'Pacific' type steam locomotives designed by Sir Nigel Gresley which until that time had been in charge of the fastest expresses running between London King's Cross and Edinburgh Waverley. They would do this because of their immense power to weight ratio and their high level of availability achieved as a result of the efficient maintenance programme operated in their three depots at Finsbury Park in London, Gateshead, then in County Durham, now Tyne and Wear, and Haymarket in Edinburgh. Expertly driven, they were soon seen travelling in excess of 100mph (161km/h) at the head of such prestigious expresses as 'The Flying Scotsman' and 'The Aberdonian', thereby reducing journey times substantially.

Following the trials carried out with the prototype Deltic, now confined to the NRM, the production fleet were introduced and numbered from D9000 to D9021, later renumbered under TOPS to 55 001 to 55 022. Outshopped in two-tone green with cream-white window surrounds they were quickly adorned with the bright yellow warning panel at each end, common to all other British diesel and electric locomotives. They would all soon receive their names. The eight allocated to Finsbury Park depot were named after famous racehorses following a tradition established by the LNER, while the six Gateshead locos and the eight to Haymarket were given the names of regiments of the British Army from the north-east of England and from Scotland respectively.

The prototype 'Deltic', DP1, now on static display at 'Locomotion', the NRM's site at Shildon.

The nameplate of Finsbury Park Deltic number 55 001 as she waits at York in February 1975. She was scrapped at Doncaster Works in February 1980.

The nameplate of Haymarket Deltic number 55 016 at York during May 1975. She was saved into preservation and is now owned by Locomotive Services Limited.

The nameplate carried by Gateshead Deltic number 55 017 at York station in May 1975. She was scrapped at Doncaster Works in January 1983.

Under the terms of the maintenance contract agreed with English Electric, that company was responsible for dealing with the inevitable teething problems encountered with these new locos and was penalised for any loss of availability in the period up to 1966. A second contract which ran until 1969 was agreed on terms more favourable to English Electric. That said, throughout the period the fleet kept running and the engine performance and reliability kept improving. After the expiry of the second maintenance contract responsibility passed to BR's Doncaster Works where an early decision was made to fit electric train heating when locos came into the works for a scheduled maintenance, a costly process and one which had to be weighed against the life expectancy of the Deltics, which had originally been estimated at ten years.

By 1973, track enhancement on the ECML had progressed to such an extent that 80 per cent of the route had been upgraded for 100mph running – an ideal stage upon which the Deltics could show their true colours and a challenge to which they would prove more than equal. They would continue as the premier motive power for passenger services between London and Edinburgh through the early 1970s until finally challenged by the Class 43 High Speed Trains (HSTs) introduced from the middle of the decade, whereupon they would be increasingly relegated to sleeper services, semi fasts and cross-country trains. It was at this time that motive power depots were undergoing a reorganisation with the stated intention of reallocating all twenty-two Deltics to York from the start of the 1979/80 timetable. However, bowing to pressure, it was later decided that Finsbury Park should keep its allocation while the fourteen stabled at Gateshead and Haymarket would be transferred to York. Finsbury Park responded by 'customising' their locos by applying white window surrounds initially to number 55 003 *Meld*. Perhaps surprisingly this unofficial paint scheme was accepted by BR's senior management and became the trademark for the Finsbury Park fleet. Not to be outdone staff at York depot responded by adding an embellishment of their own to their Deltics in the form of the city Coat of Arms, for which special permission had to be granted by the City of York Fathers.

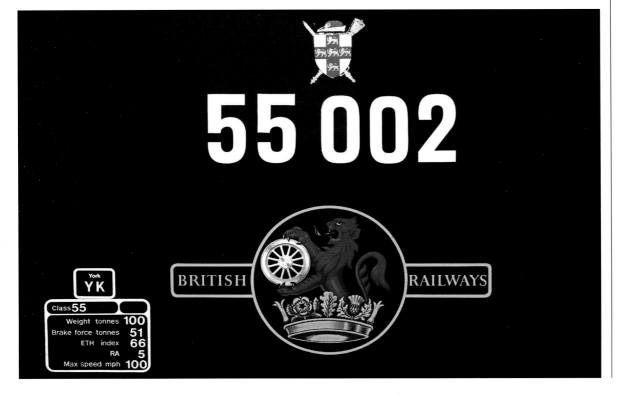

Now preserved as part of the National Collection, Deltic number 55 002 *The King's Own Yorkshire Light Infantry* carries the City of York Coat of Arms on her cab-side.

Inevitably, with their demotion from the role of first choice traction, there was more limited maintenance and failed locos were increasingly cannibalised for spare parts. First to be condemned were 55 001 *St. Paddy* and 55 020 *Nimbus* in January 1980. Number 55 002 *The King's Own Yorkshire Light Infantry* was chosen by the NRM to be preserved as part of the National Collection, but over the next two years virtually all the fleet was withdrawn. The final Deltic hauled service train was the 16.30 Aberdeen to York service on 31 December 1981, brought in from Edinburgh by 55 019 *Royal Highland Fusilier*. On 2 January 1982, an enthusiasts' special the 'Deltic Scotsman Farewell', ran between King's Cross and Edinburgh in the care of 55 015 *Tulyar* and 55 022 *Royal Scots Grey*, with 55 009 *Alycidon* shadowing the trains in each direction in case of an engine failure. The 'Deltic Era' had come to an end.

The Deltic Preservation Society (DPS) had other ideas. Formed in 1977, by 1982 enough members had joined and enough funds had been raised to purchase both 55 009 *Alycidon* and 55 019 *Royal Highland Fusilier*. By 1986 55 015 *Tulyar* had been added to their Deltic fleet along with the cab of 55 008 *The Green Howards*, this to be used as a virtual reality driver experience at their Barrow Hill Roundhouse headquarters. A second cab, that of 55 021 *Argyll and Sutherland Highlander*, is also preserved, this by the South Wales Loco Cab Preservation Group while two more locomotives have also been saved, numbers 55 016 *Gordon Highlander* (static display) and 55 022 *Royal Scots Grey* (under repair), owned by Locomotive Services Limited. Of the six production Deltics which have survived into preservation only one, 55 019 *Royal Highland Fusilier*, is currently operational.

During the heyday of the Deltics, pristine Class 55 number 55 010 *The King's Own Scottish Borderer* threads the down 'Flying Scotsman' through York station on 21 February 1975.

On 21 December 1976 Class 55 number 55 020 *Nimbus* takes 'The Aberdonian' northbound from York station.

Speeding south from York on 2 December 2011 and heading for Lincoln with the Scottish Railway Preservation Society's rail-tour, 'The Santa Express' from Linlithgow, is 55 022 *Royal Scots Grey*, here passing Colton Junction.

Restored to her original livery, D9009/55 009 *Alycidon* hurries south towards York near Beningbrough on 11 June 2013 with the returning 'The Elizabethan' rail-tour. The earlier King's Cross to Edinburgh leg had been taken by 'new-build' Class A1 number 60163 *Tornado*.

CHAPTER THREE

INTER-CITY 125s ENTER THE SCENE

By the time the first production Class 254s, Inter-City 125s or High Speed Trains (HSTs) were operating along the ECML the Deltics were already running well beyond their estimated ten-year life expectancy but even they could not compete with the next generation of express passenger trains. Initially considered to be diesel multiple units for numbering purposes, the HST sets were composed of a Class 43 power car at each end of six to nine Mark 3 coaches. Each power car was fitted with a 2,250 bhp Paxman Valenta engine giving a total of 4,500 bhp for the train (compared with the two 1,650 bhp engines of a Deltic loco) and their high power to weight ratio meant that their top operational speed of 125mph (201km/h) was easily within their capability. From the summer timetable of 1978 they were in charge of the fastest ECML expresses, including 'The Flying Scotsman', reducing the journey time between London and Edinburgh by up to thirty minutes. In 1987 a world record for the fastest diesel-powered train was set when power cars 43 102 and 43 159 attained a speed of 148mph (238km/h) while descending Stoke Bank.

Approaching York near Overton is an HST set led by 254 002 with the up 'The Flying Scotsman' in the summer of 1978.

On 24 February 1979 HST set 254 007 gets the green light at York with the 15.34 departure to Edinburgh from King's Cross. Clearly still something of a curiosity for enthusiasts.

Inter-City 125s pass at Holgate in 1988.

Now sporting the 'Intercity Swallow' livery and carrying the Class 43 number 43 195, an Edinburgh to King's Cross service rolls into York on 18 July 1994.

Following the retirement of the Deltics, the Class 254 HSTs became the chosen motive power for services between London and Scotland as well as often featuring on trains to Leeds, Bradford, Cleethorpes, Hull and Scarborough. A total of ninety-five HST sets were built between 1976 and 1982 which included 197 Class 43 power cars. They were numbered from 43 002 to 43 198 (though the original sets carried numbers beginning 253 *** for the Western Region and 254 *** for the ECML stock). Numbers 43 000 and 43 001 had been applied to the two prototype power cars, one of which is now preserved as part of the National Collection and numbered 252 001. The design proved a great success for British Rail and though the original Valenta engines were replaced from 2005 in order to extend their working lives by ten years, many have continued to give excellent service in the post privatisation era. British Rail had been in state ownership since 1948 until the operations of the British Railways Board were broken up and sold off under the Railway Act of 1993 and privatisation implemented over three years from 1 April 1994. Train Operating Companies (TOCs) then competed for franchises to run passenger trains over various parts of the network which is maintained by Network Rail. HSTs operated by TOCs including East Midlands Railway, Cross Country and Grand Central still put in appearances at York station to this day. The company LNER withdrew the last of their HSTs in December 2019 but Network Rail's 'New Measurement Train', nicknamed the 'Flying Banana', is a regular sight in the area.

On 22 December 2010, the final runs powered by an original Paxman Valenta engine took place between Sunderland and York. Still carried by HST power car number 43 123 the special train completed two return journeys 'top and tail' with number 43 468 (seen above leading towards York on Journey No.1). Though the final return from York was delayed by an hour due to a signal failure north of the station a small group of enthusiasts had assembled to see the last 'Valenta' pull away, opposite above.

The commemorative plate carried by Grand Central HST power car 43 123 as she waits at York station for her final run to Sunderland on the evening of 22 December 2010.

Virgin Trains East Coast (VTEC) operated the franchise on the ECML from 1 March 2015, taking over from the East Coast TOC in a joint venture between Stagecoach and the Virgin Group. Though intended to operate until 2023 the contract was terminated early by the government and VTEC ceased operating on 23 June 2018 when operations were taken over by the government owned London North Eastern Railway (LNER). LNER is owned by the Department for Transport and is contracted to operate services on the ECML until 2025 as well as managing twelve stations itself, including York.

A Virgin Trains East Coast set with power car 43 257 on the rear calls at York with 1E03, an Edinburgh to King's Cross service on 14 April 2015.

On 1 December 2015, VTEC Special Livery power car number 43 238 *National Railway Museum 40 Years* at the platform at York on the rear of 1E13 Inverness to King's Cross.

Now in the hands of LNER, an HST set with train 1S16, a King's Cross to Inverness service, calls at York on 20 March 2019 with power car 43 208 *Lincolnshire Echo* on the rear.

Sporting the full Virgin branding, an HST set led by 43 313 with 43 272 on the rear approaches York near Overton with 1E07, an Edinburgh to King's Cross train on 31 March 2018.

Under York station's splendid roof, a Grand Central HST set with power car 43 465 on the rear, 43 468 on the front, pauses with 1A61, a Sunderland to King's Cross train on 9 April 2015. Grand Central is a TOC owned by Arriva UK Trains and has operated passenger services between King's Cross and Sunderland since 2007 and between King's Cross and Bradford since 2010.

Leaving York having negotiated Colton Junction, a Cross Country HST set led by 43 384 with 43 378 on the rear of 1V54, a Dundee to Plymouth service on 16 June 2015. The TOC Cross Country is also owned by Arriva UK Trains and operates long-distance and intercity services across Great Britain including the UK's longest direct rail service from Aberdeen to Penzance with a journey time of more than twelve hours.

Waiting to take 1Y86, the York to King's Cross service on 20 March 2019 is East Midlands Trains HST set led by power car 43 048 *TCB Miller MBE*, with 43 083 on the rear. East Midlands Trains is owned by the Stagecoach Group based in Derby. It operated a franchise to provide trains as far as York from 2007 until August 2019 when a new franchise was awarded instead to Abellio East Midlands which is branded as East Midlands Railway (EMR) and operates out of London St. Pancras. EMR has services mainly along the Midland Main Line to Nottingham and Sheffield with extensions to Leeds and York. The franchise is due to run until August 2027.

Network Rail's New Measurement Train (NMT) approaches Colton Junction, York from the Leeds direction on 15 February 2014 led by 43 062 *John Armitt*.

Nicknamed 'The Flying Banana', the specially modified and equipped HST set operates over all parts of the network where HSTs are permitted, checking the condition of the route on a four-weekly cycle at a maximum speed of 125mph (201km/h). It has been in service since 2003 and is based at Derby. There are three Class 43 power cars available, numbers 43 013, 43 014 and 43 062, any two of which operate 'top and tail' with five dedicated Mark 3 carriages.

And finally . . . on 20 December 2019 a cheery 'whistle' and wave from the driver on a dull, wet day by the ECML near Overton as power car 253 003 heads towards York with 1Z48 the Edinburgh to Leeds, day three of four charity special 'The Northumbrian LNER HST Farewell'. In BR's blue, yellow and white livery the charter's proceeds would be in support of LNER's partner charity 'Campaign Against Living Miserably' (CALM), leading a movement against male suicide.

An unexpected pleasure – a ScotRail HST set led by 43 143 with 43 179 on the rear races north from York on 28 November 2020 as train 566H, Doncaster Works Wabtec to Slateford Depot, Edinburgh.

CHAPTER FOUR

EXPRESS FREIGHT HAULAGE

By the 1970s, the expanding motorway system had dealt a severe blow to BR's dated freight network, so much so that urgent reform was needed if the railways were to compete successfully for the lucrative long-distance express freight contracts being increasingly awarded to road haulage companies. The days of mixed-traffic locomotives capable of hauling passenger or freight trains were coming to an end as it was realised that freight needed to be fast, efficient and reliable, delivering the goods at speeds comparable with those of passenger trains. Bigger, purpose-built freight locomotives hauling new high-capacity goods vehicles would be needed to achieve this goal. Extending the Total Operations Processing System (TOPS) into the freight sector would allow the more efficient use of rolling stock thereby reducing costs while at the same time the more efficient service would attract more business and so generate more income. Increasingly the use of containerised handling systems as recommended earlier by Beeching in his report 'The Reshaping of British Railways' published in 1963 would be a major factor contributing to the revitalisation of the freight network as it would shift the emphasis away from 'wagon-load' traffic handled at marshalling yards to long distance bulk transport often employing intermodal containers.

In the 1980s, BR was reorganised in an attempt to reverse the continuing serious decline in freight traffic, but it was not until the privatisation of BR in the 1990s that the fruits of increased competition and the resulting greater reliability were seen in the form of a sharp increase in the amount of freight carried on the railways. Companies at the forefront of this rail-freight revolution include several whose locos are frequently seen on the lines through York with either intermodal (container) or train-load freight which might be coal (declining rapidly), oil, metals or construction materials. The four main operators are currently Direct Rail Services, Freightliner, GB Railfreight and the largest, DBCargo (formerly EWS). In addition, the smaller operators Colas Rail and DCRail are regularly encountered in the area. Increasingly major retailers including Asda, Tesco, Morrisons and Marks & Spencer are moving their goods by rail, while the growing concern about the environment has seen increased traffic in the form of 'energy from waste' trains. International traffic has also increased since the opening of the Channel Tunnel in 1994.

Class 56

A fleet of new diesel express freight locos was needed to bring about this rebirth of the rail freight business. At the forefront was the Class 56, a design based upon the Brush Traction Class 47 bodyshell with an engine developed from that used in the English Electric Class 50. A total of 135 locos were built between 1976 and 1984 and though the first thirty sub-contracted to Electroputere in Romania were poorly constructed and had to be withdrawn from service early for rebuilding, they and the remaining 105 built by

British Rail Engineering Limited (BREL) at Doncaster and Crewe Works would prove to be powerful and reliable locomotives, being used extensively by EWS amongst others until the mid-1990s when withdrawals began. As of 2018, a total of thirty-five were listed as either operational or in store, the main owners being GB Railfreight (with eighteen examples listed), Colas Rail (ten) and DCRail (three). Most of these have re-entered main line service after having been purchased for preservation and only three are technically 'preserved', being 56 006 owned by the Class 56 Group and based on the East Lancashire Railway, 56 097 operating on the Great Central Railway (Nottingham) and 56 301 also owned by the Class 56 Group but on spot hire to British American Railway Services (BARS) who also operate formerly preserved 56 057 (renumbered to 56 311) and 56 091 under their Devon and Cornwall Railways (DCR) subsidiary.

Class 56 number 56 090 leaves York avoiding line with empty coal hoppers and heads for the north east during the 1980s.

A short time later, sister loco number 56 072 follows with a similar load.

Leaving York station in the mid-1980s is Class 56 number 56 074 *Kellingley Colliery* with a scrap metal train. Built in March 1980, withdrawn in September 2010 and sold to European Metal Recycling (EMR) at Kingsbury, she was saved and reinstated in November 2014 although she has since been withdrawn again. *Douglas Todd*

Passing the site of the former Bolton Percy station and approaching York on 4 December 2012 is Devon and Cornwall Railways Class 56 number 56 311, formerly number 56 057, at the head of train 6Z58, the Cheddleston to Stockton scrap metal working.

Waiting at York Holgate Sidings for a path on 4 July 2013 is the now preserved Class 56 number 56 301 with scrap metal empties. Formerly number 56 045 she was overhauled and refurbished by Brush Traction, purchased by the Class 56 Group and is here on hire to Devon and Cornwall Railways.

Class 60

During the 1980s, BR recognised the need for a large fleet of powerful 'Type 5' diesel electric freight locomotives and invited tenders for their construction and delivery. The contract for 100 locomotives was awarded to Brush Traction and these were subsequently built, with the first being delivered in June 1989 with construction continuing until 1993. They were designated BR Class 60 and numbered 60 001 to 60 015 (60 016 was renamed from *Langdale Pikes* to *Rail Magazine* and renumbered to 60 500 in November 2004 to commemorate the 500th issue of *Rail Magazine*) and 60 017 to 60 100. All members of the class were named, most after British hills and mountains or famous British citizens, though several were renamed in subsequent years.

Following the privatisation of BR, all 100 engines were acquired by English, Welsh and Scottish (EWS) who continued to operate the fleet until 2007 when they were taken over by DB Schenker, a subsidiary of Deutsche Bahn. They were used extensively to haul heavy trains of construction materials, petroleum and steel. From 2010 a number of locos were sold on to DC Rail and to Colas Rail who subsequently sold them to GB Railfreight, GBRf. The first of the class to be withdrawn was 60 006 *Great Gable* in January 2020, while three have so far been preserved, numbers 60 050 *Roseberry Topping* and 60 086 *Schiehallion* on the Wensleydale Railway and 60 081 *Bleaklow Hill* (later renamed *Isambard Kingdom Brunel*) by Locomotive Services Limited.

Leaving York and heading south on the ECML with a train of EWS petroleum tanks under threatening skies on 30 August 2012 is DB Schenker Class 60 number 60 079 *Foinaven*.

In support of a Network Rail P-way gang track-laying at Holgate, York on 16 December 2012 is DB Schenker Class 60 number 60 040 *The Territorial Army Centenary*.

Still carrying her EWS livery on 17 October 2013 is Class 60 number 60 071 *Ribblehead Viaduct*, seen here near Colton Junction with a train of empty 'flats' from Tees Dock to Aldwarke (Rotherham).

Approaching Colton Junction, York on 15 February 2014 is DB Schenker Class 60 number 60 099 *Ben More Assynt* with a north-bound steel train. In 2010 she was painted into TATA Steel's silver livery at Toton TMD.

Leaving the outskirts of York on 28 September 2018 in Colas Rail Freight livery is GBRf Class 60 number 60 047 *Robert Owen* with train 6H70, Tyne Coal Terminal to Drax Power Station.

Class 66

When BR's freight operations were privatised in 1996, 93 per cent of the business was bought and controlled by Wisconsin Central Transportation Systems who named their UK company English, Welsh & Scottish (EWS). Needing to replace their ageing diesel fleet the new company placed a large order for 250 new locos, later to be classified as Class 66, with builder Electro-Motive Diesel (EMD), an American locomotive manufacturer owned by Caterpillar. The first units arrived in early 1998 and proved so successful that orders soon followed from other Freight Operating Companies (FOCs) including Freightliner, GBRf and DRS. Later EWS including its French subsidiary Euro Cargo Haul were bought out by DB Cargo UK who continue to operate the fleet of Class 66 locos.

Without a doubt the most frequently observed diesel freight locomotives passing through York is this highly successful and reliable addition to the UK's freight fleet with 550 examples being introduced in the UK since that first delivery in 1998. They are numbered in several series between 66 001 and 66 957, nicknamed 'sheds' by enthusiasts, a reference to their 'end-on' appearance, and continue to be operated by the major rail-freight companies including Colas Rail, DB Cargo UK, Direct Rail Services, Freightliner and GBRf, though following the run-down of the coal-fired power stations at Ferrybridge and Eggborough, together with the conversion of Drax from coal to more use of biomass, their frequency at the head of trains in the York area has declined markedly in recent years.

The last Class 66 delivered to the UK was in the Spring of 2016 when GBRf took charge of number 66 779, appropriately named *Evening Star*. Like its predecessor the Class 9F steam loco number 92220 it was accepted by the NRM to be part of the National Collection, but not until the end of its working life, which could be in as much as forty years' time. For the present, this large and ubiquitous class with its several operators can inevitably be seen in a number of liveries, though it is the GBRf fleet which displays the most variation.

Heading a coal train from Tyne Dock to Drax PS on 3 February 2012 is 'rainbow' liveried 66 720. The design was the winning entry in a competition held the previous year to find a bright and original livery for a GBRf Class 66 loco.

Passing Shipton by Beningbrough and approaching York on 27 December 2019 is 'the last one', GBRf Class 66 number 66 779 *Evening Star* with sister loco 66 780 *Cemex Express* in tow. Number 66 779 was painted in BR Brunswick Green with BR logo as the last of her class of 700 locos built for the UK and European markets and imported from the USA between April 1998 and May 2016. Unveiled at a ceremony in the NRM, York on 10 May 2016, she was named *Evening Star* to remember the last steam locomotive built for BR in March 1960, Class 9F number 92220, which was withdrawn from service into preservation a mere five years later. GBRf CEMEX liveried classmate number 66 780 is one of ten former DB Cargo locos sold to GBRf in December 2017 and then modified to sub-class 66/7 and renumbered accordingly. Number 66 008, the first of the ten, became 66 780.

Carrying the livery of the Swiss international shipping line the Mediterranean Shipping Company on 8 October 2013 is GBRf 66 709 *Sorrento* as she heads away from York with a Tyne Dock to Drax PS coal train.

Passing Colton with a Tyne Dock to Drax PS coal train on 20 May 2014 is 66 721 *Harry Beck* carrying the livery 'GBRf Supports the London Transport Museum'.

Approaching York on the ECML on 15 December 2018 in the livery of Biffa Waste Management Services is GBRf 66 783 *The Flying Dustman* with train 4N80, Doncaster Down Decoy to Tyne Coal Terminal.

In the distinctive livery of Colas Rail Freight is Class 66 number 66 848 heading away from York for Drax PS with her coal train from Tyne Dock on 19 February 2013.

Passing Copmanthorpe on the western outskirts of York on 14 June 2014 with an engineers' train is DB Schenker Class 66 number 66 152 *Derek Holmes, Railway Operator*.

Approaching York with 435S, the Leeds FLT to Tees Dock FLT container train on 24 May 2016, is Freightliner Class 66 number 66 528 *Madge Elliot MBE*.

Heading north on the ECML from York and passing Shipton by Beningbrough on 4 July 2017 is DRS Class 66 number 66 424 with train 610G, Mountsorrel Sidings to Carlisle loaded ballast, via the Tyne Valley line.

Passing Colton Junction with 'the blue train' on 3 May 2018 and still in EWS livery is Class 66 number 66 006. The working is 632A, Wilton Energy from Waste Terminal to Knowsley Freight Terminal.

Five coupled Freightliner Class 66s trundle north from York on 28 November 2020 as train 0945, Leeds Balm Road to Millerhill S.S. light engine movement, led by 66 597 *Viridor*, followed by 66 570, 66 615, 66 528 *Madge Elliot MBE, Borders Railway Opening 2015* and finally 66 514 bringing up the rear.

Class 67

The BR Class 67 diesel electric locomotives were built in Spain between 1999 and 2000 for EWS, totalling just thirty in all. In the York area they are most often encountered as 'Thunderbird' rescue locos for failed trains on the ECML, though examples may appear on freight workings or more likely at the head of charter 'specials' as they are able to supply electric train heating and air conditioning and are capable of high-speed running up to 125mph (177km/h). They are known as 'skips' to enthusiasts. Most of the fleet are now operated by DB Cargo UK though two were sold by them to Colas Rail in January 2017 (numbers 67 023 and 67 027) to be used by Network Rail as infrastructure monitoring trains.

EWS Class 67 number 67 028 sets off southwards from York along the ECML on a Thunderbird rescue mission on 6 March 2014.

Heading north towards York on 19 June 2014 is DB Schenker Class 67 number 67 015 *David J. Lloyd* in Wrexham & Shropshire's silver and grey livery. Five locos formed this sub-fleet which was created in 2008 but dispersed at the end of 2014 when they were repainted according to their new roles.

Approaching Colton Junction on the ECML south of York on 20 July 2016 is DB Schenker Class 67 number 67 018 *Keith Heller* at the head of 134V, the London Victoria to York Belmond British Pullman. She carries the 'Maple Leaf' livery and name in honour of the Canadian-born former EWS and DB Schenker UK chairman.

Class 67s numbers 67 023 *Stella* with 67 027 *Charlotte* on the rear with the Network Rail temporary measurement train on 31 March 2018. Once a year the two Class 67s operated by Colas Rail Freight stand in for the New Measurement Train when the HST set is out of service for maintenance. They are seen here heading north from York and passing Shipton by Beningbrough with 149H the Derby RTC to Heaton T&RSMD, the set including Overhead Line Test Coach number 975091 behind the leading loco.

Called into action in place of steam loco Class A1 number 60163 *Tornado* which had become unavailable due to 'mechanical issues', DB Schenker number 67 018 *Keith Heller* brings 1Z63, the Scottish Railway Preservation Society 'The York Excursion' rail-tour from Linlithgow to York via the S&C towards the city on 3 November 2018, later to return north by way of the ECML.

Awaiting her next 'Thunderbird' rescue duty in the 'Parcels Sidings' at York station on 11 August 2016 is DRS Class 68 number 68 003 *Astute*.

Class 68

The thirty-four locos of Class 68 are a diesel-electric mixed traffic design built for DRS in the UK. Numbers 68 001 to 68 009 and 68 016 to 68 018 continue to be operated by DRS, used mainly on container traffic, nuclear flask trains and contracted Network Rail duties, while six locos are sub-leased to Chiltern Railways (numbers 68 010 to 68 015) and the remaining sixteen sub-leased to TransPennine Express (TPE), being numbers 68 019 to 68 034, though the last two numbered locos remain in DRS livery and are used by TPE as back-up as and when required. The first batch was built by Vossloh Espania during 2013 to 2015 with further batches by Stadler Rail being delivered between 2016 and 2017. Capable of running up to 100mph (161km/h) and carrying electric train heating equipment the DRS locos are regularly seen in the York area on 'Thunderbird' rescue duties while those later sub-leased to TPE are used as the driving force for their 'Nova 3' train sets introduced into service in 2019.

Class 70

Though rarely seen in the York area other than when passing through as light engine movements, the thirty-seven Class 70 freight locos were built by General Electric in the USA. Numbers 70 001 to 70 020 are operated by Freightliner Powerhaul and numbers 70 801 to 70 817 by Colas Rail Freight. They are designed to be an improvement on the ubiquitous Class 66 freight locos having air conditioning and acoustic insulation for crew comfort, increased 'crashworthiness' and greater fuel efficiency.

Freightliner Class 70 number 70 011 passing Dringhouses on 19 December 2020 as 057U, a light engine move from Leeds Balm Road to York Yard South.

Out of the Vale of York mist running as 029Q Carlisle New Yard to Doncaster Carriage Holding Sidings, come Colas Rail Class 70s numbers 70 812, 70 806 and 70 817 passing Shipton by Beningbrough and approaching York on 7 November 2020.

CHAPTER FIVE

ANGLO-SCOTTISH ELECTRICS – CLASS 91

By 1982, the InterCity 125s (IC125s) had displaced the mighty 'Deltics' on the ECML, over which the fleet had held sway since the 1960s when they had ousted Sir Nigel Gresley's illustrious A4s in the run-up to the end of steam on the East Coast route. During this period, the journey time from London King's Cross to Edinburgh was reduced from around eight hours to a little over four and a half hours. The electrification of the ECML to York in 1989 and onward to Edinburgh completed in 1991 paved the way for the introduction of electric traction between King's Cross and the Scottish capital. With overhead wires now in place, enter the InterCity 225 (IC225), a high-speed train comprising a 25kV Class 91 electric locomotive at the north end, a set of usually nine Mark 4 coaches and a Mark 4 Driving Van Trailer (DVT) at the London end. This enabled the train to be propelled from the rear while being 'driven' from the front on return journeys by means of cab controls which replicate those of the Class 91. Their power output of 6,300bhp clearly out-muscles the Class 254's 2x 2,250bhp which in turn left the Deltic, once the most powerful single unit diesel locomotive in the world, far behind with 2x 1,650bhp. Britain's fastest railway locomotive would reduce the journey time between the two capitals to an impressive four hours, give or take a minute or two.

The plan to produce a train capable of running at speeds up to 225km/h (140mph) took shape and the design brief was put out to tender resulting in GEC Transportation Projects being employed to manufacture the electrical equipment, BREL sub-contracted to build the body structure and fit out the locomotive and Metro Cammell contracted to build and supply the rolling stock. Building on the experience gained from the demise of the Advanced Passenger Train (APT) project and the highly successful IC125s a total of thirty-one sets were produced between 1988 and 1991. The Class 91s were originally classified as 91/0 and numbered 91 001 to 91 031, though when refurbished by Adtranz/ Bombardier at Doncaster during 2000 to 2002 they were reclassified to Class 91/1 and renumbered 91 101 to 91 122 and 91 124 to 91 132. Number 91 023 had been involved in both the Hatfield and the Great Heck rail crashes and after its refurbishment in 2001 it was given a new identity and hopefully a change of fortune as number 91 132. The thirty-two DVTs carried the numbers 82 200 to 82 231. With a design capability of 140mph (225km/h) they were easily capable of the line speed of 125mph (201km/h) and indeed a speed of almost 162mph (260.7km/h) was recorded on a test run in 1989 on Stoke Bank between Peterborough and Grantham.

Over the following thirty years after the Class 91s entered service, each locomotive completed on average almost eight million miles, or about 700 miles per day. Though never fully realising their potential to run at their maximum design speed due to speed restrictions on the ECML the last passenger locomotives built for British Rail undoubtedly proved themselves worthy successors to the earlier speedsters.

Following the privatisation of BR, the fleet was sold to Eversholt Rail Group who subsequently leased them to operators of the InterCity East Coast franchise, which has included Virgin Trains East Coast (VTEC) and more recently from 2018 London North Eastern Railway (LNER). They continued to dominate the ECML high speed operations until May 2019 when the first Class 801 'Azuma' trains entered service allowing the InterCity 225 sets to be withdrawn and returned to Eversholt for possible re-leasing to other Train Operating Companies (TOCs). However, seven sets have had their lease extended by Eversholt until 2023 and possibly into 2024 and continue to work the East Coast route beyond their proposed withdrawal date of June 2020, though none should be running north of York after September 2020. It remains to be seen if the impressive Azuma fleet will achieve the mileage clocked up by the 91s of more than 244 million miles, the equivalent of almost 10,000 times around the world!

In recent years, individual Class 91 locomotives have carried notable special liveries including number 91 110, holder of the record for Britain's fastest locomotive at 161.7mph, which carried the insignia of the Royal Air Force Battle of Britain Memorial Flight and its three famous Second World War aircraft, the Spitfire, Hurricane and Lancaster. Number 91 111 was named *For the Fallen* in October 2014, the centenary year of the outbreak of the First World War, and carried the distinctive livery depicting images relating to that conflict and to the five regiments along the East Coast route that fought in the Great War. Number 91 119 was repainted in the original InterCity-style livery at Bounds Green and named *Bounds Green InterCity Depot 1977-2017*, while 91 101

One of the first for York. Class 91/0 number 91 014 *Durham Cathedral* is providing the power for this Edinburgh to King's Cross service on 18 July 1994.

carried the purple branding and *Flying Scotsman* motif and 91 107 was renumbered to 91 007 to promote the James Bond film 'Skyfall', the 007 livery 'wrapped' with a set of Mk4 carriages and unveiled at King's Cross on 16 February 2013. Finally, for Christmas 2015 number 91 128 and a DVT were decked out in a festive livery by Virgin Trains East Coast and named *Intercity 50*.

Class 91/0 number 91 021 *Royal Armouries* in original Intercity livery waits at York with a train for Edinburgh on 19 October 1996. Built in October 1990 she was later re-named to *Archbishop Thomas Cranmer* and renumbered to 91 121 when the Class was redesignated to 91/1 during the refurbishment which took place between 2000 and 2003 following the acquisition of the fleet by the Eversholt Rail Group as a consequence of the privatisation of British Rail.

Hurrying towards York at Colton Junction on 11 February 2014 is VTEC special liveried Class 91 number 91 110 *Battle of Britain Memorial Flight* at the head of a King's Cross to Edinburgh service.

In East Coast silver livery, Class 91 number 91 102 *City of York* races away from the city near Shipton by Beningbrough on 15 November 2014 with 1S18 King's Cross to Edinburgh.

The nameplate carried by Class 91 number 91 102 *City of York*.

Calling at York on 21 June 2018 with 1E07 Edinburgh to King's Cross is VTEC special livery Class 91 number 91 111 *For the Fallen*.

Detail from the livery of 91 111 at York on 21 June 2018.

On the rear of 1S14 King's Cross to Edinburgh as it leaves York on 15 December 2019 is LNER DVT number 82 205 in *Flying Scotsman* livery.

One of the last Class 91 services to run north of York calls at the station on 24 September 2020 as 91 105 takes 1S08 King's Cross to Edinburgh, with DVT 82 211 on the rear. In March 2021 came the news that withdrawals of Class 91 locos had begun and that fourteen examples taken out of service were being stored at Doncaster and Leeds Neville Hill. First to arrive at Sims scrapyard, Beeston on 18 March was number 91 132 which as well as being the first of the class to be scrapped had previously been involved in the fatal accidents at Hatfield in October 2000 and just four months later at Great Heck, after which it was renumbered from 91 023 following refurbishment in 2001. Three more of the class, numbers 91 103, 91 104 and 91 108 which have been used as parts donors, are also expected to be scrapped in the near future.

Reliving the years of Intercity livery, LNER Class 91 number 91 119 *Bounds Green Intercity Depot 1977 – 2017* is on the rear of 1E09 Edinburgh to King's Cross at York on 15 December 2019.

CHAPTER SIX

STEAM HAS NEVER BEEN FAR AWAY

The official 'end of steam on BR' came with the ban on steam traction imposed from 12 August 1968 following the last main-line passenger train to be hauled by steam power, the so-called 'Fifteen Guinea Special' on 11 August, though by the autumn of 1967 steam in the Yorkshire area had all but disappeared. York North shed 50A officially closed to steam at the end of June 1967 and on the penultimate day of that month it was home to a collection of diesels which included English Electric Type 1 numbers D8300/1/5/7/8/9/11 and 12, BR Type 2 number D7569, English Electric Type 3 number D6794, Brush Type 4 numbers D1102/3 and English Electric Type 4 numbers D250/256/270 and D278. Steam seen on shed at this time included B1 4-6-0 numbers 61030 *Nyala* and 61337 together with privately preserved A4 4-6-2 number 60019 *Bittern*. Withdrawn locos still housed in the shed on that date included K1 2-6-0 numbers 62001 and 62065, BR 3MT 2-6-0 numbers 77002 and 77012 and B1s numbers 61012 *Puku*, 61019 *Nilghai*, 61021 *Reitbok*, 61123, 61189 *Sir William Gray* and 61337. The last outposts for steam were Bradford Low Moor still holding on to the last of the LNER B1s until the end of September and Leeds Holbeck with a couple of Jubilees and a few Black 5s still operative into October. Preserved A4 Pacific number 60019 *Bittern* housed at York North shed could occasionally be seen working RCTS charter 'specials' into November, with the Manchester Rail Travel Society's 'Mancunian' from Leeds to Carnforth and Manchester advertised as the engine's last run on 25 November 1967.

Such was the love of steam traction amongst railway enthusiasts and the wider general public that these symbols of our industrial heritage were not allowed to pass into extinction. The railway preservation movement was taking shape nationally and steam was at its heart. Locomotives were bought and lovingly restored, some having been withdrawn from service several years before, and an army of volunteers appeared to convert hunks of rusting metal into working 'iron horses' once again. In West Yorkshire the Keighley & Worth Valley Railway re-opened as a preserved line as early as June 1968 while in North Yorkshire the North Yorkshire Moors Railway Preservation Society was formed in 1967, though fare-paying passengers being carried across the lonely moors by steam train did not become a reality until 1973. By this time BR's management were beginning to realise that steam had appeal (and therefore money to be made) with the result that the 'steam ban' was gradually lifted and BR itself became involved in the operation of main-line steam trips.

In the York area, the 'Yorkshire Circular', later to be re-routed and named the 'Scarborough Spa Express', was one such early BR venture launched in the 1970s and proved so successful that it still operates. At one time the only steam loco allowed to run over BR metals after the 'end of steam', former LNER A3 number 4472 *Flying Scotsman*, was an early recruit to promote BR's Yorkshire Circular tour which ran from York through Leeds to Harrogate and back to York. Other notable 'regulars' included Class V2 number 4771 *Green Arrow* and later LMS Coronation Pacific number 46229 *Duchess of Hamilton*, A4 number 4498 *Sir Nigel Gresley*, SR West Country Class number 34092 *City of Wells* and BR 9F number 92220 *Evening Star*.

As Class 45 number 45 134 stands at the platform with her Plymouth to York excursion on 7 April 1979 she is passed by LNER V2 number 4771 *Green Arrow* with 'The Northumbrian' rail-tour. Originating at King's Cross the tour had been brought to York by Class 55 Deltic number 55 003 *Meld* whereupon the steam-hauled section was advertised as York to Carlisle and return. However, as a result of the Penmanshiel Tunnel collapse on 17 March and the consequent lack of paths resulting from diversions, the steam section became a 'mystery tour' which took the form of a circular trip including Knaresborough and Sheffield before the Deltic returned the train to King's Cross.

Approaching York at Clifton Bridge on 8 July 1979 is LNER A4 number 4498 *Sir Nigel Gresley* at the head of the 'Yorkshire Circular' rail-tour, having just left the Harrogate Branch, while HST power car number 254 005 is on the rear of a King's Cross to Edinburgh express.

Heading the 'Yorkshire Circular' tour in August 1979 is LNER A3 number 4472 *Flying Scotsman*, here passing through the former station at Long Marston on the approach to York from Harrogate.

By the 1980s it had become clear to all that steam hauled special trains were a major attraction and could generate much interest and revenue. By this time, BR's Scarborough Spa Express had become a summer season 'regular', having extended the 'Yorkshire Circular' route to include a trip to the coast. Here SR Lord Nelson Class 4-6-0 class leader number 850 *Lord Nelson,* the only preserved example from the class of sixteen built between 1926 and 1929, eases past Bootham level crossing signal box with the returning train from Scarborough to York on 12 August 1981.

Not the best of weather for a trip to Scarborough as Coronation Pacific number 46229 *Duchess of Hamilton* leaves York in the rain with the Scarborough Spa Express on 18 August 1983.

The last steam locomotive to be built for BR, Riddles 9F 2-10-0 number 92220 *Evening Star*, manoeuvres into position at York station to head the Scarborough Spa Express in the 1980s. Built at Swindon Works in March 1960, she had a pitifully short working life for BR, being withdrawn in March 1965 having been destined for preservation from the start. After withdrawal and restoration at Crewe Works, she took her place in the National Collection though continued working on loan to the Keighley & Worth Valley Railway. After a period based at the NRM in York she worked for a time on the North Yorkshire Moors Railway and finally the West Somerset Railway until 1989 when she was installed as a static exhibit at the NRM. She was subsequently displayed at the NRM Shildon and at Swindon Steam Works to celebrate their Fiftieth Anniversary before returning to the York museum in 2010.

Since those early tentative steps, the steam preservation movement has grown from small beginnings largely inspired by a handful of dedicated amateurs to become a major industry run on a professional footing and though all 'heritage railways' still depend heavily on their faithful volunteers their working is delivered to the highest of standards. Today there are close to 120 standard and narrow-gauge heritage railways operating in England alone while on the main lines steam can be seen at work at the head of charter specials throughout the year. The charter train 'industry' is estimated to contribute £30 million to the economy annually.

Leaving York behind with 1Z44, the Railway Touring Company's York to Carlisle via Leeds railtour, 'The Waverley' on 7 July 2019 and passing Colton Junction is LNER A3 number 60103 *Flying Scotsman*.

Attracting an admiring crowd at York station on 27 July 2019 is LMS Jubilee number 45596 *Bahamas* having arrived with 1Z18, the Vintage Trains Dorridge to York 'The White Rose'.

Steaming well as she approaches Colton Junction and York with 1Z34 'The Christmas White Rose' from Dorridge on 14 December 2019 is GWR Castle number 7029 *Clun Castle*.

Racing through the site of the former station of Bolton Percy between York and Leeds on 8 September 2019, SR Merchant Navy class number 35018 *British India Line* heads 1Z44 'The Waverley' towards Carlisle by way of Leeds.

Entering York station on 24 September 2020 is LMS Jubilee number 45699 *Galatea* running as long gone classmate 45562 *Alberta* in charge of 1Z24, the final 'Scarborough Spa Express' of the season. The train had been brought in to York from Carnforth by two WCRC Class 47s working 'top & tail', which after leaving the coaches in Holgate Sidings to be united with the Jubilee were themselves parked in the station's Parcels Sidings, below.

WCRC Class 47s numbers 47 772 *Carnforth MPD* and 47 802 are seen parked in York station's Parcels Sidings alongside DRS Class 37 number 37 402 on 24 September 2020. The Class 47s will take the Scarborough Spa Express back to Carnforth following the completion of the steam-hauled leg of the journey to the coast.

CHAPTER SEVEN

AZUMA AND NOVA

After several years of indecision, the Department for Transport finally launched the Intercity Express Programme (IEP) in March 2011 with the intention of procuring replacements for the InterCity 125s and 225s with new express fleets composed of trains built to three specifications: overhead line electrically powered, self-propelled and a 'bi-mode' version, to operate on the East Coast and Great Western main lines. The contract to supply the new fleet was won by Agility Trains, a consortium which includes Hitachi, and which was formed with the sole purpose of bidding for the IEP. The new trains are based on the Hitachi 'A-train' design and form part of the AT-300 family. They are assembled at the company's Newton Aycliffe facility from bodyshells shipped over from Japan. The AT-300 intercity high speed and long-distance train is part of a family of modern designs which also includes high density urban trains (AT-100), suburban, commuter and regional trains (AT-200) and high-speed 'Bullet' trains (AT-400).

The UK was the first country outside Japan to place a major rail order when Southeastern (London & South Eastern Railway Limited) bought twenty-nine Class 395 'Javelin' sets which entered service in 2009. Later the AT-300 family in the UK was enlarged by the addition of the Class 800 electro-diesel 'bi-mode' units and the Class 801 electric multiple units, branded as 'Azuma,' which would become familiar in LNER livery through York, and the Class 802, branded as 'Nova 1' sets, operated by TransPennine Express (TPE).

THE AZUMAS – 'EAST' MEETS WEST
The ECML trains entered service in May 2019 carrying the brand name 'Azuma', the Japanese word for 'East', with the first Anglo-Scottish departure being the Up 'Flying Scotsman' on 1 August of that year. Previously test trains in Hitachi grey livery could regularly be seen in the York area and it was during these 'trial-runs' that it was discovered that the units created electro-magnetic emissions which interfered with lineside equipment including signals, thereby delaying their entry into public service until the problem was solved. In the meantime, the testing and driver training continued only in diesel mode.

Today LNER operates its sixty-five Azuma sets between London King's Cross, north east England and on to Edinburgh, Glasgow, Aberdeen and Inverness using both electric and bi-mode versions. The fastest journey time between the English and Scottish capitals is four hours and between London and York is one hour, fifty-one minutes. The Class 800/1 bi-mode fleet consists of thirteen nine-car sets and ten five-car sets numbered 800 101 to 800 113 and 800 201 to 800 210 respectively, while the Class 801/1 electric multiple unit (emu) fleet consists of twelve five-car and thirty nine-car sets numbered 801 101 to 801 112 and 801 201 to 801 230 respectively. Each emu set also has a diesel engine fitted for use in an emergency. They are maintained at the LNER depots at Bounds Green, Doncaster Carr and Craigentinny.

VTEC Azuma bi-mode set led by number 800 101, the pre-production set built in Japan, running as 5X71 empty coaching stock test train from Doncaster Carr Depot to Edinburgh on 30 January 2018 approaching York at Colton Junction.

Cab end detail of 800 101 approaching Colton Junction on 30 January 2018.

An unusual visitor to York on 30 January 2018 were GWR bi-mode sets composed of 800 003 *Queen Victoria* leading 800 004 *Isambard Kingdom Brunel* here leaving Colton Junction with 5X32 empty coaching stock test train from Darlington to Doncaster.

Running in diesel mode as 5X22 empty coaching stock test train from York to Peterborough and leaving Colton Junction on 14 August 2018 in unbranded grey livery is five-car Azuma set 800 201.

Now in full LNER branding, nine-car Azuma set 800 110 races towards Colton Junction and York on 3 August 2019 with 5Q21 Peterborough to York empty coaching stock for crew training.

Having arrived at York from King's Cross, coupled LNER Azuma five-car sets number 801 101 and 801 104 wait to take the return as 1Y84 on 6 March 2020.

At York on 6 March 2020 LNER Azuma emu set 801 207 leaves with 1E07 Edinburgh to King's Cross as TPE Nova 3 1E29 arrives from Liverpool Lime Street destined for Scarborough led by Driving Trailer number 12812 with Class 68 number 68 021 *Tireless* out of sight providing the power from the rear.

THE 'NOVA' FAMILY

At about the same time the TOC TransPennine Express (TPE) was introducing its own versions of the new trains under their brand name 'Nova'. TPE is owned by First Group and operates intercity services from Liverpool Lime Street and Manchester which call at York en route for Scarborough or north east England. From August 2019 the Nova fleet appeared first in the form of 'Nova 3' sets comprising a Class 68 diesel loco, Mk 5A coaches and a Driving Trailer on the remote end from which the set can be driven using a cab layout similar to the Class 68. Fourteen five-car sets are operative with two spare locos being available from DRS if required. The locos are numbered from 68 019 to 68 032 and are able to run at up to 100mph (161km/h). Though built by Hitachi the sets are maintained by Alstom in Manchester while the locos are essentially a mixed traffic design owned by Beacon Rail and leased from DRS.

Having passed through Colton Junction on 30 December 2017, DRS Class 68 number 68 031 *Felix* is on the rear of the York to Liverpool leg of the Deltic Preservation Society charter 'The Trans Pennine Deltic Lament'. Leading the way is Deltic number 55 009/D9009 *Alycidon*.

In the Scarborough bay platform at York on 11 January 2019 is TransPennine Express Class 68 number 68 020 *Reliance*. A number of these locos, leased from DRS, have been in use regularly for driver training in preparation for the introduction of Nova 3 passenger services later in the year.

Arriving at York on 15 December 2019 is 1F66, a Scarborough to Liverpool Lime Street service led by TransPennine Express Driving Trailer number 12812. The power on the rear is supplied by Class 68 number 68 028 *Lord President*.

Having brought in 1T60 from Scarborough on 15 September 2020 Class 68 number 68 034 awaits the return from York. One of the two 'spare' locos drafted in from the DRS fleet along with 68 033, number 68 034 is standing in as none of the TPE fleet were available.

These were followed a month later in the York area by the bi-mode Class 802/2, branded 'Nova 1'. These nineteen 5-car sets are capable of 125mph (201km/h) working and operate services between Liverpool Lime Street and Edinburgh via Newcastle and between Manchester Airport and Newcastle, running in electric mode where possible but able to continue on unelectrified routes using their diesel generator engines. They replace the Class 185 'Desiro' sets and are numbered 802 201 to 802 219. They are maintained by Hitachi in Doncaster and Edinburgh.

The Class 802s are virtually identical to the Class 800 Azuma bi-mode trains operated by LNER except that the Novas operate with a higher engine power and are fitted with a larger fuel tank to enable them to cope with the gradients and extended running in diesel mode over the long unelectrified routes on which they operate. Like the Azumas, change over between modes can occur at line speed and in both versions two five-car sets can be coupled to form a longer train if needed.

Hurrying along the ECML north from York on 9 November 2019 is TPE Class 802/2 Nova 1 set number 802 212 with 9E09 Liverpool Lime Street to Newcastle.

TPE Nova 1 set number 802 217 pauses at York on 10 September 2020 with 1P75, a Manchester Airport to Redcar Central service.

Pulling away from York ahead of its Azuma equivalent on 10 September 2020 is TPE Nova 1 set number 802 218 with 1P27 from Liverpool Lime Street to Newcastle.

To showcase speed and style through the ages and to celebrate the heritage and future of one of the country's most iconic railway lines, this unique event which took place on 23 April 2017 saw four generations of East Coast traction forge their way side-by-side along the main line towards York. Organised jointly by Virgin Trains, Network Rail, the National Railway Museum, Hitachi and 'Welcome to Yorkshire', preserved Gresley A3 Pacific number 60103 *Flying Scotsman*, Hitachi 'Azuma' Class 800 set 800 101, VTEC Class 225 set led by DVT number 82 205 in *'Flying Scotsman'* livery with 91 105 on the rear and VTEC HST set 43 238 *National Railway Museum 40 Years 1975-2015* with 43 290 *MTU Fascination of Power* set off together from Tollerton. They are seen here alongside the Sidings Hotel, Shipton when the East Coast Main Line was closed temporarily to enable this special event to take place. *Rick Ward*

FUTURE PLANS

Major works under consideration for the future include plans for a series of major upgrades on the York to Newcastle section of the ECML in preparation for the planned arrival of HS2 and High Speed North trains in the 2030s. The proposals include a major rebuild of the station and junction at Northallerton and additional platforms at York and Darlington. Four additional platforms would be built at York in order to create increased capacity, with the former bay platforms one and two removed by BR in the 1980s being reinstated for local trains while platforms twelve and thirteen would be added at the western side of the station for through traffic. In addition, a third track would be included between York and Skelton Junction where the Harrogate line diverges. By early 2021 work on the first stage of the £600m Trans-Pennine upgrade of the route between York and Manchester was visible at Colton Junction in the form of masts for the Overhead Line Electrification and troughing for the associated new signalling equipment, all this is in addition to work already underway to improve the 25kV AC power supply north of Doncaster in order to allow more electric trains to operate in future, as at present some TransPennine Express Class 802 bi-mode sets have to work in diesel mode north of Newcastle due to power supply issues.

Improvements to facilities at York station include the provision of a new Travel Centre on the main concourse with the old Travel Centre being used to accommodate two new retail outlets. A lounge for First Class passengers was also due to be completed early in 2021. These and other projects are being developed in close cooperation with City of York Council with a strong focus on retaining original layouts and features in keeping with the station's Grade II* Listed status. Major changes are planned for the front of the station including the demolition of Queen Street Bridge, built to cross the long since removed railway lines which ran through the City Wall into the old station. A new layout is proposed giving access to a re-designed station portico along with development of the Railway Institute Gymnasium area, while at the opposite side of the tracks the National Railway Museum is due a 'face-lift' both inside and out alongside a controversial plan to develop adjacent railway land for residential and commercial use as part of a major regeneration scheme for the area around York's historic station. Exciting times lie ahead for York and its ever-evolving railway, as, never content to rest on its laurels, the challenges of today and tomorrow are met with enthusiasm and enterprise.

BIBLIOGRAPHY

Harris, Michael (ed), *This is York, Major Railway Centre,* Ian Allan, 1980

Hoole, K., *The Railways of York,* Dalesman, 1976

Hucknall, David, *British Diesel Locomotives,* The History Press, 2012

Longworth, Hugh, *British Railways Steam Locomotives 1948-1968,* Oxford, 2013

Marsden, Colin J., *Rail Guide 2020,* Crecy, 2020

Marsden, Colin J. & Fenn, Graham B., *British Rail Main Line Diesel Locomotives,* Oxford, 2000

Mather, David, *The Railways of York,* Silver Link, 2014

Myler, Chris, *The Life and Times of York Carriage Works 1884-1995,* ABB Rail/The Amadeus Press, 1996

Rose, Peter, *Railway Memories No.5; Return to York,* Bellcode Books, 1994

Ross, David, *British Steam Railways,* Paragon, 2003

Speakman, Colin, *Transport in Yorkshire,* Dalesman, 1969

Vaughan, John, *The Rise and Fall of British Railways; Main Line Diesel Locomotive,* Haynes, 2011

Wolmar, Christian, *Cathedrals of Steam,* Atlantic Books, 2020